CHILDREN OF THE ANCIENT ONES

CHILDREN OF THE ANCIENT ONES

BY LITTLE PIGEON

Herald Publishing House, Independence, Missouri

COPYRIGHT © 1982
Little Pigeon
Independence, Missouri

All rights in this book are reserved. No part of the text may be reproduced in any form without written permission of the author, except brief quotations used in connection with reviews in magazines or newspapers.

Library of Congress Cataloging in Publication Data

Little Pigeon, 1913-
   Children of the Ancient Ones.

   1. Indians of North America—Addresses, essays, lectures. 2. Little Pigeon, 1913-   —Addresses, essays, lectures. 3. Indians of North America—Biography—Addresses, essays lectures. I. Title.
E77.2.L55   1982   973'.0497   82-11745
ISBN 0-8309-0344-5

Printed in the United States of America

Contents

		Page
Introduction		7
Prologue		9
Chapter 1	How to Be Happy Though Indian in a White Man's World	13
Chapter 2	On That First Book	29
Chapter 3	Journey into Light	37
Chapter 4	The Culture	48
Chapter 5	On Identity	61
Chapter 6	The Image	74
Chapter 7	This Old House	86
Chapter 8	The New Heroes	93
Chapter 9	Home Is the Hunter	102
Chapter 10	Of Indian Blood	108
Chapter 11	The White Suitcase	116
Chapter 12	Indian—and Christian	127
Chapter 13	Fourteen—with Love	144
Chapter 14	Outrageous Fortune	155
Chapter 15	A Land Shadowing with Wings	167
Chapter 16	—And Rainbows	176
Chapter 17	So Now You Know	193
Chapter 18	Reveille at Paint Creek	203
Chapter 19	The Eagles Are Gathering upon the Land	207
Chapter 20	For the Healing of the Nations	214
Epilogue	The Kingdom	224

INTRODUCTION

During the past twenty-five years or so, as I have traveled about this fair land, I have been impressed by the myriad questions asked by people of all ages and persuasions about American Indians. The millions of Americans who claim some Indian heritage, school children and their teachers, and visitors from other lands are intrigued by the history and culture of this unique people. While it is true that many of the questioners were still caught up with the "tepee and tomahawk" image, and viewed the subject from a standpoint of what they thought the Indian *ought* to be, there is an increasing awareness that we who are Indian also have graduated into the twentieth century.

It was to answer some of these questions that this book grew into being. It does not attempt to speak for *all* Indians for they, like other people, have had various experiences which affect their feelings and reactions to any issue.

Particularly in the Restoration church, so long and so vitally concerned with a ministry to this "remnant people," it is, I think, equally vital to gain some understanding of the peculiar problems and rationale of those with whom we hope to communicate.

There are some bitter memories here, and I have heard it said that we should exorcise the sorrier events of our past and view only the happy and more spiritual aspects of a people obviously preserved by God for his purpose. This is like telling a gardener that he should ignore the weeds and view only the harvest. The buried traumas of childhood cause painful inadequacies in adult lives; only by getting them to the surface of consciousness can they be healed. The world should never forget the Holocaust, if for no other reason than that, left unchecked, humankind is capable of terrible deeds. We should, I believe, be watchful sentinels upon the walls, that by the grace of God working through our intelligence and compassion, such things will never happen again.

Still, Indians do not get up each morning to chalk a mark in the air and say, "Today I will think about the issues." It is my hope that in rambling through the years covered in this book with this sometimes ludicrous Indian caught up halfway between the old world and the new, you will emerge with a deeper understanding and love for my beloved people.

Little Pigeon

In 1946 Little Pigeon was married to Grey Owl, a descendant of a long line of traditional chiefs. It was a second marriage for both of them. They began with a ready-made family — her two and his five — then added seven, including two sets of twins.

At the time of Grey Owl's death in 1959 the older children were grown; the younger ones were still at home and thus intimately involved with the events of this book. All the members of this remarkable family are very special people, full of talent and charisma. Nine of them have served voluntary enlistments in the armed services, and most of them are now following careers in government.

Although only three of the children are mentioned by name in this book, all are very close in spirit. The life of each would require another volume, and they all agree that the focus of attention in **Children of the Ancient Ones** *should be on the issues facing Indian people... and the unfolding of the Master's plan in these latter days.*

Prologue

At odd moments over the years I thought that someday—if I ever finished darning socks and paring potatoes—I would write a book; and what I had in mind was a book of essays. I had been enchanted with essays since the week we read Stephen Leacock in high school. This should give you some idea of how many years ago *that* was!

When you stop to think about it, the first person narrative is very good therapy anyhow. I was born with an invidious temper and learned by experience that there was much more effective discipline in writing my complaints than in counting to ten. Then, of course, as I began to get out in the world, I found that no one was really interested in my tantrums; I had no audience. Very often, reading over the biting sarcasm; the monumental and (I thought) righteous anger I had dashed off a week ago was a bit like reading last year's yellow-sheet journalism—much ado about nothing. Still, it was enlightening to know how I had felt at one particular point in time. I expect that other people have had similar experiences.

Take Indians for example. Indians are—as are other people—often filled right up to the eyebrows with searing wrath. We don't just get angry, we get doggone mad; but, like other people, we often translate that wrath into terms we can live with. For example, the BIA with its stultifying bureaucracy is sometimes referred to in the wigwam as the "Bureau Where Indians Have Their Affairs," our often fumbling attempt at cross-cultural understanding as "Racy Relations." We sulk in majestic silence, or we smash things, or we storm City Hall. And sometimes we are so overcome with the utter nonsense of it all, we agree, as grandpa used to say: "Might as well quit and go rabbit huntin'."

Long ago I concluded that smashing windows was ineffective; people just call the insurance company. Still, you have to admit that something is wrong between us, for all that we try. And I'll let you in on something right now—many Indians don't communicate with each other any better than they do with folks outside the neighborhood. Even when we share the same language, or know enough English that it becomes a workable tool, we sometimes just don't get through to one another.

I am convinced that many people—even more than Indians could guess—really want to know about their red brothers and sisters who, of course, are not "red" in any sense of the word. I accumulated this impression through twenty-five years of answering questions. What the questioners wanted to know was not so much "What's happening?" as "How do Indians feel about it?" What turns them on—or off? So I thought I would spell it all out, both for my own therapy and as a sort of historical record in case we get wiped out of existence — which is not as farfetched an idea as you might like to think.

In order to do this effectively, I ought to tell you something of the way I operate, so that no one a hundred years from now will get the impression that I'm penning this thing on a log beside the campfire.

Years ago, before I began to write in earnest, I pictured myself approaching my desk of a morning all crisp and cool, sharpening the day's pencils, and setting to work with brisk efficiency. What usually happened was that I would fritter away the day doing all sorts of trivial, ineffective things, postponing the final confrontation. But as soon as I gave up and went to bed, ideas and words would begin to cavort through my brain like mice; my eyes would absolutely refuse to close. I would crawl out of bed to grope... not for the desk but for the kitchen table.

It's a firm rule in this house that any notebooks not totally filled in the classroom automatically belong to mama. I do not think that any of my young people took notes beyond the third class lecture, for there seems to be an inexhaustible supply of copybooks bearing copious notes over the first six to eight pages, and nothing beyond. There is no method in this madness; I seem to work in five or six notebooks at once. One book may hold a rough draft of a letter to my sister-in-law, pages of very shaky shorthand with a heading, "Shawanese Traditions," grocery lists, addresses of schools, half an article for a magazine (the other half is in another notebook).

Now here is a page that ought to give pause to some grandchild on a faraway rain-filled afternoon:

Visitor has come with box of relics. Among them tiny tomahawk head. Was it toy for child? Old man shows it to boys admonishing them to handle with care.

I have no idea what I had in mind when I penned those cryptic notes, but immediately there follows this list.

Hardboard paneling for library. 12 sheets, check cost.
Remove porch roof; concrete floor
Aluminum pillars?
6 fruit trees: 2 peach, 2 plum, 2 apricot
Move couch and chair.

Now it may seem strange that moving a couch and chair should be included with such monumental plans as propping a porch or laying a concrete floor. As a matter of fact, the repositioning of furniture here is more unlikely than undertaking a repair job that has been hanging fire for ten years. The couch and chair will probably remain in status quo while I yet live. To move them might mean I'd break my neck getting to the kitchen on one of my nightly sorties; for, with the best intentions in the world, I have found that writing seems to grow on one—and day after day provides new things to write about.

Still, it's a humbling experience in the end. I might start with the elevating thought that by the waving of my magic pen I will solve the problems of hunger, of crime in the streets, shifty politics *et alles*...and I wake up Monday morning to find that the world is just as hungry, there have been as many muggings, and quite as many oily political promises.

So I come down from my high horse and begin to write for the sheer joy of feeling the scratch of a pen on paper—and the hope that somewhere along the line, some thought or feeling or experience will touch one other soul in whatever particular crisis is being faced.

This for the essayist is the moment of truth. Whether it's nobler to suffer in the mind the slings and arrows or (with apologies to Shakespeare), to take arms with pen and copybook and purge the soul in one outpouring of the spirit.

And what I really mean to say is that for *my* people, as for any others, life is not all "beer and skittles" (whatever *that* may be) but neither is it all slings and arrows. It's a rollicking, rib-tickling, tear-jerking, browbeatin' mishmash of skittles and slings—and rainbows.

CHAPTER 1

How to Be Happy Though Indian in a White Man's World

Once upon a time I wrote an unpretentious little gem called How to Be Happy, etc. which I came across while clearing the accumulation of ten years' junk in my battered old file case. It is of interest only in that—looking back after spending the biggest part of twenty-five years in this outside world—I am amazed at the changes that have taken place.

Above all, I am amazed at our unmitigated gall. Were my husband and I ever so naïve as to set forth on a crusade with zero cash and fourteen children? Apparently we were, for that's where the story opens.

Actually, we didn't plan it that way. We weren't trying to be heroic or to get our names on the Wampum. When we came to Detroit in 1949 it was just an adventure—a chance to make some money, to "live like a white man."

It was just that we loved our people with a love so deep, so tall and wide we found ourselves viewing each new experience through their eyes.

Well, that's true enough still. The love remains though the captain of this crew is gone. The experiences we had those years ago were real enough and still could happen, magnified by new problems, modified by new circumstances.

It is something to remember that we were so "green" we did not know that when a man went to work the members of his family stayed at home or occupied themselves in other ways. Where we came from—and in that time—there simply was no work for Indians except farm labor. We worked in tobacco or picked tomatoes or pulled flax. Whatever it was, most likely the whole family went along. Sometimes the women worked to double the income; sometimes they didn't. Children ran free, following their fathers in the rows, or tumbling about the camp where kettles of corn soup bubbled. It was hard work, and the summer's wages represented the entire yearly income, so it was never possible to get out of the rut of waiting for the next season.

There was something precious about it, though, and there was always a lot of laughter, of running races or holding dances in the evening.

Now, remembering those first terrifying weeks in the city with its constant streams of traffic, ear-splitting noise and flashing lights, I recall most keenly the sense of loss and uncertainty when we finally realized there was to be this separation of the family. People thought there must be something very wrong with a man whose wife and children followed him to work and sat for eight hours waiting for the whistle to blow.

Well, that much has changed somewhat. Finding a job is a little more complicated today, and the outside world has thrown its shadow into reservation lands sufficiently to have provided plenty of "separation" before we emerge.

Another thing that has constituted a difference is that to most Indians of our day, as a sad commentary on what it meant to "live like a white man," was the idea that we could buy a drink legally. There was a law that imposed stiff penalties for selling liquor to Indians and stiffer penalties still for Indians caught with the stuff in their possession.

Indians with the cash could always buy the liquor, but the thing to do was to get rid of the evidence, so they drank it as fast as they could get it down. "Living like a white man" meant that they could get a drink with less effort, but there was that ingrained uneasiness, so they tore into the bottle as though dying of thirst, and often dashed out for the next bottle before someone would happen to remember to close the gate.

Now this law has gone the way of other unenforceable legislation, so there is no longer such an excuse, and Indians, if they drink, do so for the same reason anyone else does—because they want to.

One of the discoveries we made in those first months was that a lot of the homefolks who had dropped from sight were to be found in a worse rut than the one they had hoped to leave. It is not certain that every Indian is aware of this, but there is a curious custom out here that not only makes alcoholics but makes fools of the celebrants as well. The custom is the idiocy of competitive drinking. Its chant is "First I'll buy one, then you buy," taken up by a chorus of "Are you going to buy one or be one?" Obviously you are eligible only as long as your cash holds when your participants stumble off to look for another "live one."

My "old man," as most of us respectfully designated our partners in life, drove a delivery van in

Detroit for a time. He had an understanding employer who thought it would be sensible to let us use the van on weekends to take the children for an outing or to go to Farmer's Market, which we did. It was, however, also my husband's little weekly contribution to park at Third and Michigan (otherwise known as Skid Row) at two o'clock on a Saturday morning. There he would gather up those of his people who were a little the worse for wear and at least take them to a place of safety. For those who maintain the bars simply work at a trade; they are certainly not going to be responsible if patrons get themselves knocked on the head in an alley. As for those "drinking buddies," friendship often ceases at 2:00 A.M.

We were indeed fortunate to observe this phenomenon early on so that there was going to be no such cloud on *our* horizon when we set out on what we called our great experiment.

The city, for all its noise and ugliness, was fascinating in a way. At night while the younger children slept, we set the oldest on watch and tramped the streets to window-shop and marvel at all the things that human hands had made. I can't remember that we ever really wanted any of them—we only marveled at the lengths to which imagination and skill of hand could go.

It was on such a night the thought came to us, as it had come to others no doubt, that somehow our people must learn to live with this—that the white people are here to stay. And we faced that ultimate uncertainty. Would we be able to retain our identity in the midst of an overwhelmingly pressure-filled world?

The most important thing to an Indian is to be Indian. We don't want to be white or even a good copy. We would rather not be a *poor* Indian, but if there was a choice between being a poor Indian and a rich anything else, we'd be poor. No one has to remind us that our heritage is a proud one. We know it.

Still, even in that far-off time before it was fashionable to be "ethnic," we realized that we would have to make *some* concessions if we were to get along "out here." The trouble was, we didn't know what they would be.

We sensed that there was something different in our approach to life but couldn't quite define that difference. We dressed as did anyone else within our means; ate more or less the same foods if we could get them. If there was a dance on the Reservation, it would most likely be a square dance. And yet—there was something alien to us in these people rushing along the city streets.

In the long hours of that night all these questions came to us and we began to consider how we might get some answers. We began to realize that we were fairly typical of our people at that time. We had rudimentary educations but no job skills. We talked fluently with our own groups but found it very difficult to talk to strangers. Our major concern was somehow to hold our family together, not just physically but spiritually. Perhaps the experiences that came to us in this new world might come to others of our people. It was important to know what our reactions to these new conditions would be.

At that time in Detroit there were roughly 3,000 Indians. They were not always the *same* Indians, but the number remained fairly constant. We tended to congregate in certain areas so that we were insulated to a degree. If we were to learn anything about being "Indian in a white man's world" we would have to get out of that safe cocoon and into a place where there were no others of our people to bolster our courage.

So, with no fanfare, we rented a truck, loaded up our children, our beads and baskets, and took to the Fair circuit looking for the place that would say, "This is your destination."

In late years when people ask why we chose to come to Ohio, they look at me uncertainly when I say we would come to a crossroads and I would fling out an arm in any direction and say, "That way." One direction was as good as another.

The miles from Detroit to central Ohio were long and hard with a truck full of children. We were weary, tired of searching, and ached with loneliness for our own kind of people. Here in this part of the country, the spirit of our ancestors was very strong. Here was Flint Ridge where the Great Spirit had laid bare the breast of Mother Earth so that her red children might take the material for their knives and arrow points. Here was the giant earthwork that was, we had been told, a veritable Holy of Holies to ancient ancestors. Here was a measure of the peace we had known at home. Life moved more slowly, though to a different drum.

There were no Indians...just miles upon hundreds of miles of farms and villages, towns and cities full of "white-eyes." We felt like a tiny island in the midst of a vast sea, and we viewed our neighbors warily. What we knew about the white people was not promising. We had heard all the tales of the sad old days and the promise of "new legislation" that came to naught. We knew what it was to gather with friends of an evening and to have the police crash the party to see what we were doing. We knew that if an Indian made one misstep the penalty was swift and drastic, and that simply being visible made one vulnerable to incarceration on suspicion.

It was some time before we realized that our neighbors were equally wary of us. Indians were unpredictable—like the grizzly. Indians lived in tepees, which would be incongruous in the neighborhood and lower property values. Most fearful of all, Indians scalped people. Mothers were holding telephone consultations on the advisability of allowing their children to go to school.

This whole mess of misunderstanding was cleared up by a kitten. The kitten appeared in our yard one morning, and my husband—who loved all animals and wanted to impress his children to look out for them—picked the wee thing up and, a half-dozen of his own crew at his heels, strode across the street to return it to the pink house where it lived.

The lady inside gave one horrified gasp to see this big Indian bearing down on her abode. She had barely time to hook the screen and retreat to the farthest wall.

"I found your kitten over there," said the fierce warrior, "I thought it might get hit by a car..."

The lady dissolved in gales of hysterical laughter. The story was retold with embellishments and the cloud of fear over the community began to lift. Obviously an Indian who had more concern for the safety of a kitten than he had for scalps couldn't be all bad. They were still not convinced about Indians in general, but "their" Indian was friendly.

On our part, we were learning something new about white people. Obviously they were not all lolling in the lap of luxury while our people starved. They had to shop just as carefully for bargains as did we; they were just as likely to have their lights shut off as we were if they couldn't pay the electric bill. In fact, in some ways, it was very difficult for them. If a job was lost, the rent and taxes went on just the same. There was no place for them to "hibernate" to wait for the coming of the next season.

Many of the men had a consuming dream. They longed to revert to the wilderness, to get away from the constant pressure and to pit themselves against more natural exigencies.

It was sometimes embarrassing for my husband.

"I always wanted to get off in a big stretch of woods with nothing but a knife and just live by hunting and fishing," they would say. "How about I pick you up, Chief, and we take us a month down in the West Virginia mountains?"

Now my husband had once made his living as a hunter, and being too poor to afford a rifle and ammunition, he had eked out an existence with a club and his wits. He knew how, but it seemed a poor sort of vacation to him. His idea of a real vacation would have been a luxury suite at the Hilton with breakfast in bed.

Still, with the easing of tension, we were getting along fairly well. One thing that helped, I believe, was that we had obedient children. When we pointed out the boundaries of our little property and cautioned them not to reach for the neighbor's strawberries, they obeyed—a fact that was impressive to the neighbors and raised Indians a degree in their estimation.

We had decided that no matter how difficult the task, we would answer questions as factually as we could; for in that way we might learn just what were the danger areas of opposing customs.

The word "squaw" is anathema to our people of the East. It has a strictly clinical meaning applied to a portion of an animal's anatomy but is a filthy word to apply to a human being. We wasted a great deal of time trying to correct people on this point without injuring their feelings, since they appeared to think they were flattering us by talking Indian. At last we concluded that we certainly couldn't rewrite all the books and movies from which they had learned the word, and if they wanted to "talk dirty" that was their business.

Our perception became sharpened until we could tell to an exact degree the sincerity of interest on the part of questioners, and we learned when to drop the subject short of senseless argument about unimportant details.

The question at the top of the list in the category of being the most invariably to be expected was "Are you a real Indian?"

It is probably a sign of the times that when that question finally descended upon a son in his high school years, he replied with some asperity, "No, I'm plastic."

We had a terrible time financially, having no marketable job skills and little experience. Besides, we had come out of a culture which had ground into us certain laws and principles:

Thou shalt not be too pushy.

Thou shalt not vaunt thyself or boast about thy accomplishments.

Thou shalt, in modesty, not be quick to speak, but shalt be observant if another's need is greater than thine own.

Lofty principles, but they do not help you get employment in a highly competitive society. My husband had the good fortune to stumble into a job in an automobile plant in Detroit, and we envisaged a brilliant and lucrative career. However, within a month he was on sick leave more often than he was at work. We learned that he was one of the people who could not adjust to factory conditions. The noise and the pace were nerve shattering. Within a month he had dropped thirty pounds; in two months he jumped if I dropped a plate. So he drove a truck for a year, and the skies fell. In a routine checkup he was found to be diabetic—and that was that. Afterwards he held a series of temporary jobs, and this was traumatic.

It's very hard now to remember how difficult it was just to approach someone about employment. The more often it happened, the more self-esteem he lost, and there were so many forms and questionnaires. When, at last, he was faced with the most complicated of all—and for a job which might have been permanent—he broke down and answered a question in a way that was entirely truthful for him, but not guaranteed to make a favorable impression. The question was:

"Do you speak a foreign language; if so, identify."

He answered: "Yes. English."

So it was that we came at last to depend on our handcrafts—a delightful way of life but not one which "bringeth forth riches."

We missed the homey excitement of cousins dropping in at odd hours, the good feeling that comes from the knowledge that we are all in the same boat and have to help one another. To our surprise, however, we learned that a lot of the same sort of thing goes on in the outside world as well. That first Christmas, which was going to be a rather slim time—but not as slim as some we had known—a truly beautiful thing happened.

The cars and trucks began to roll up to the house on December 24. In a steady stream, it seemed, baskets and boxes of food began to descend the little path and to pile up in the kitchen and finally to overflow into the parlor. We had never seen so much food in a private home or such an endless variety.

We strove to remember who had brought which baskets but were overcome by sheer numbers. Sunday school classes, the Boy Scouts, the local PTA—these we could understand, for we knew that dispensing

Christmas cheer was one of their happier projects—but most of the gifts were from single families or individuals who "just happened to have a little extra."

The climax came when the ladies from the local church brought a deliciously cooked dinner, saying, "You've had so much company, we thought you wouldn't have had time to get supper."

We were stunned. My husband's English deserted him completely; he reverted to his own language and pronounced a blessing on the food that threatened to have us eating supper at six o'clock in the morning.

Where were the white people who hated Indians?

We were so impressed that we tried very hard to improve our own conduct and value in the community, a fact that I strongly suspect added to the cementing of relations. The time was to come that if we did encounter discrimination or bigotry, we were able to view it as an isolated case rather than to attribute the condition to the race as a whole.

By the time 1959 rolled around we felt so knowledgeable about conditions in the outer world we were ready to go home and share that knowledge. We hadn't the slightest intention of superimposing white economy and culture on the reservation, for we had found much that was uncomfortable to us. There was too much rush, too much pressure, too much concrete, too much dog-eat-dog competition, and we wanted none of that for our people.

Still, there were some really good things which might increase to a degree our enjoyment of life without our sacrificing Indian values.

The long hunt of the winter was over now. Gone were the days and weeks of preparation for the major preoccupation of the year. The winter nights were long and cold with little to do except to sit close to the fire.

We had discovered a rare joy in reading, and for the first time in our lives there was an inexhaustible supply of reading material. Books were a charmed council circle where the adventuresome and wise of all ages shared their tales of valor or wisdom. Someone had told us, too, that every year or so many fine books were culled from the libraries, and it was suggested that almost anyone was happy to give a book to a worthy cause.

So one of our most cherished dreams was to start a lending library on the Reserve. In Indian fashion, it wouldn't depend on fancy buildings or degrees in library science. There would simply be the books and somewhere a room in which to put them. No doubt it would be good training for the young people to dispense them and keep simple records.

A more ambitious plan was to start a community center (and I smile now as I recall our modest ideas in that more innocent time). Many of our people had just about given up raising a garden except for a few vegetables to eat in season. We were too poor to afford canning equipment or jars in which to put the vegetables we might raise. Why not a community kitchen? Why not suggest to those eager-to-help people who "wanted to do something" to let us have the fruit jars they no longer used now that they had supermarkets and freezers?

Today, of course, these things are being done on a larger scale than we could have imagined, but I think the thing that most enhanced our enjoyment was considering these adaptations that might help our people. To share with one another, to use wisely the fruits of the earth for the good of all—these were a most precious part of the wisdom of our fathers.

Our plans, of course, were not to come to fruition, for Grey Owl, the beloved, was called to a heavenly adventure—no doubt to besiege his Lord and the angels with the same questions he was trying to resolve on the earth.

I wish his people could have experienced the love poured out to us when he was laid to rest. Hundreds of white people came—not in curiosity to see whether he was buried in regalia (he was) but to tell us in so many different ways, "This man touched our lives, and we are glad."

Now that there are urban Indian centers, Indian congregations, and unrestricted Indian gatherings, our people need not feel the loneliness and isolation from each other that we imposed on ourselves. But I think that to be happy though Indian in the white world we must be willing not only to accept love when it is offered but to expect love, which is an entirely different thing—not making a "federal case" of it if a new-found friend proves false, but to smile and say, "That's life," and try again. We must cease to lump all other people outside our charmed circle into one fixed concept; we must regard one another as individuals—good, bad, and indifferent—for the whole world wasn't made to dance to our drum.

Above all, perhaps we should bring with the rest of our baggage the same good manners we practice on our neighbors at home.

It seems very sad to me that there is more bitter feeling against Indians where our population is most concentrated than there is in areas where we are few in number. I have spent a great many years puzzling over this, for our experience in the outer world has brought us rich friendships and kindly neighbors.

There have been unpleasant incidents, of course. My one excursion into the working world was a brief period in a restaurant kitchen. One customer stalked out in anger, refusing to have a "dirty Indian" involved in the preparation of his food. My employer jovially thanked her lucky stars for the loss of his patronage, since he had been an irascible customer at best.

Among the several explanations that have been advanced for the rancor against Indians in concentrated doses, two stand out as particularly ugly. Both of them are true. In the area of the reservations, there are often also powerful business interests to which the Indian holdings are a thorn in the side. If some of our people are sitting on a potential coal field or occupying a slice of coveted rangeland with no desire to have their property dug up or covered with concrete, obviously they are "standing in the way of progress." There is no way to deny that this situation exists; it is a fact of life that every reservation Indian lives with.

On the other hand, we have terrible problems with alcoholism. We can scream to high heaven about individual freedom and make all the excuses in the book; it is unpleasant for people in adjacent towns to have Indians lying drunk on a sidewalk or causing a disturbance. Naturally, the same may be said for anyone else in like condition. A degree of difference in the public attitude may lie in the fact that community drinkers are nearer their homes and their unsavory condition may be more easily concealed. Indians, in for a night on the town, still have the miles home to negotiate; hence an alcoholic condition is more visible.

Both of these reasons are going to have to go by the board. We are moving closer to firm legislation giving Indian people greater control over their own lives and property. An increasing awareness on the part of the general public, and an awakening regard of other cultures, will make it very difficult for secret pressures to be brought to bear as they have been in the past. Increasingly, too, Indians are beginning to wake up to the fact that alcohol has caused more problems than it has assuaged. More Indian communities are undertaking programs toward the eradication of this sad malady.

Incidentally, the old myth that alcohol affects Indians more severely than it does non-Indians is just that—a myth. (Note to Indians who think they may as well have the game as the name: Sorry, you have no special talent along those lines.)

Recent studies at the Central Oklahoma American Indian Health Council and the National Institute of Arthritis, Metabolism, and Digestive Diseases (Phoenix) show that there is no biological difference in the effect of alcohol on the two groups. What is beginning to show up in clinical research, however, is that many Indians have a total intolerance for sugar in any form.

"How to be happy" is an aim we share in common with all human creatures; and it is no insipid little catch phrase that we have in mind. It involves no castles in the air, no dreams of empire, but the soul-enriching joy of living which comes from the knowledge that we fit comfortably into our environment, whatever our habitat may be.

Once, while driving a country road in Ohio, I saw against the sky a grove of hemlocks—free and tall and proud they were, isolated and alien to the quiet stretch of farmland. They are a landmark to all who travel there—"Turn right when you see the hemlocks." I thought again about my people, for we have been taught from ancient times to take our lessons from nature. Here we are, transplanted into a new environment, and it has been a hard adjustment. Now, our roots planted firmly in the beloved earth, we spread our branches wide and lift proud heads to the blessing of sun and wind. Free and tall and proud we stand—a little alien and out of place, perhaps, but a landmark to all who travel here in this time of cynicism and jaded appetite.

After the pain comes the healing; after despair, the clear, bright hope. To the uttermost bounds of the earth, wherever humankind is torn by fear and doubt, the infinite promise that where the spirit is strong and true, we *can* survive, with each one's special, unique nature intact.

As we regain our sense of self-worth and dignity as human beings, we shall be able to move gracefully in and out of this "white man's world." The world of the Indian is truly different, not so much in different goals (for both seek an improved quality of life) but in ideas of what that quality should be. Both "worlds" contain elements of beauty. It is often more difficult to convince Indians that there is anything good on the outside than it is to convince white people of the reverse.

One thing is apparent; unless we learn to love this land and cherish it, demanding the very best of ourselves that we can be, there may conceivably come a time when both worlds are lost to us. This is our Father's house, his earthly mansion where his children must abide within his law of love, enjoying the privacy of their own campfires but learning to share their joys and sorrows as his great extended family comprising many clans.

CHAPTER 2

On That First Book

I have never seen any statistics on the subject, but it would be my guess that to 75 percent of the population the idea has occurred at some point in their lives that they ought to write a book. And why not? Every human being has a story to tell. There is just no way to live on this planet without being touched by joy or sorrow, by pain or pleasure.

If one were to live isolated on the highest mountain or the most barren desert, one's life would be touched and molded by the struggle to survive. The good feeling of security that comes with game well-hung, a woodpile stocked against the cold, the welcome patch of shade beneath the sun might well be a success story. The vagaries of weather, illness, or accident faced alone present dramatic crises; the tale's conclusion, one of humankind and God in harmony through the bonds of earth and sun and spirit.

Walk the streets of the inner city and tales of raw courage, tragedies of defeat unfold. The immigrant ghettos produce a Sholem Asch. Some of the greatest stories ever told were of quiet lives moving serenely from seedtime to harvest and back again. So far as that goes, there is high drama in the world of nature—stories in stones and in every creature that creeps or walks or flies.

Thus, to imagine that one has something to write about lifts one not at all above one's fellow creatures. In fact, to actually write the book may propel the writer into the most harrowing, the most exhilarating, the most humbling experiences imaginable.

To get back to personalities—as was my intention all along—I began to write, what was much later to become a book, in the modest notion that it was something I was jotting down for my own instruction, or at most for the benefit of my children and possibly for those Indians who might be interested. There was the loneliness as a spur, and the comfort in remembering Grey Owl's infinite knowledge of his people; but I wanted to do more than simply retell the old tales. I wanted proof—at least one piece of recorded evidence—that the tales were based on fact.

So I betook me to the libraries and plowed through countless tomes describing massacres and "the real Indian way of life." The impression being hammered in by all these books was that twenty-five or thirty thousand years ago "the Indians" (lumping them all together) came across the Bering Strait and settled down to chip their inevitable arrowheads or weave their typical baskets, and there they sat for thousands of years, waiting for the white man.

Something didn't jibe, for I remembered rituals and fireside tales that told a different story. These ancient secrets handed down, held as a last bulwark to our annihilation as a people, haunted me. I began to search more diligently for truth; and having once suspected where the search was leading, I became afraid, for surely many more brilliant scholars had searched before me and found nothing more than primitive savagery in the race.

And then that giant hand reached down to shake me and the words began to leap under my pen. Oh, there were times I'd pound my fists and mutter, "Unbelievable!"—and sometimes I would drop beside the bed and pray, "Let me not write from vain imagination. Give me truth!"

By this time, of course, I had ceased to be at all modest about my aims and purposes. I wanted my people to share in the exciting things that I had found; and I wanted to shout to all the world, "Hey! Look at us! We're beautiful!" So, taking my slim courage in my hands, I mailed a sample here and there expecting—and getting—a few rejection slips, but always with some kind words, a ray of hope.

And *then*—oh, miracle of miracles, oh day of skyrockets and bombshells—a publisher nodded assent, and we were off on high adventure, my book and I.

I had had odd fleeting moments all those years in which I speculated on just what I would do if the miracle happened—if I ever *should* finish the book, and if it ever *should* be accepted. As it turned out, what really happened was surprising even to me. I opened the envelope and drew out the contract, tastefully bound in blue. I glanced at it just long enough to identify it, then walked very deliberately into the bedroom. I knelt beside the bed and smoothed the paper flat as though presenting it on a teacher's desk...and burst into tears.

"We did it! Oh, dear Lord, we did it!"

Then I cried myself to sleep.

Of course, that was just the beginning. I would have thought, if I had thought of it at all, that when a book was written the publisher did something mysterious with it and from there on, all the author had to do was to sit back and collect the fortune that would undoubtedly ensue. The truth of the matter was very far from that simplistic picture.

Rechecking references, listing a bibliography, rewriting—why, it was almost like doing the whole book over again. In an increasing humility of spirit, I now understood why so many authors include in their introductions an expression of gratitude to their editors. The pruning of commas alone must have been a formidable task!

Then there was the fumbling attempt to write a brief biography—a more difficult chore than writing the book. Brief it was sure to be, for it now occurred to me that there had been no outstanding achievements to record. I had been a very ordinary woman, all too briefly a wife, an often hesitant and uncertain mother. Caught between the dearth of education and the necessity to earn a living, I had simply done as any red-blooded woman would have done—the best I could. As for accomplishments, what on earth can one achieve while rearing fourteen children? Proud as I was of this accomplishment, my success could be reduced to one line: I helped to rear them.

Caught up in this unaccustomed routine where a deadline for the first time in my life became the essence, the thought of possible reward totally left my mind. For at this particular phase of the game, a new and unfamiliar obstacle appeared in the end zone.

Clothes!

There may have been—in some dim, long-forgotten area of my past—a time when I was concerned with hemlines, styles, and colors. That would have been, of course, before the fourteen children with their healthy appetites, their penchant for outgrowing shoes, and their unbelievable talent for losing one of each pair of socks.

It may also have been a quirk of self-abnegation, compounded by a stringently restricted budget, but the fact remained that, for many years, I had given not one breezy thought to wardrobe. The buckskins constituted my one claim to glamor, but they certainly couldn't be worn consistently day after day. A few shapeless cottons passed on from a kindly source did well enough for house and garden. Writing required no special uniform; a flannel wrapper from a son's college days was warm and comfortable.

Nevertheless, somehow I would have to come up with a decent rag or two, for a perfectly marvelous, if mysterious, thing was about to happen. The publisher spoke of an "author's reception," an "autograph party," and other assorted goodies, and I was to fly to Independence for "a busy schedule."

Now I am as sensible as the next one, and though I had never seen, must less taken part in, an "autograph party" I had serious doubts about appearing anywhere in a flannel bathrobe.

It was at the very last moment, like the cavalry riding over the hill to the sound of bugles, that the check arrived. It was actually a very modest check, surely not the retirement fund I had envisioned in my salad days. To be perfectly frank, I didn't recognize it as a check at all. I took one glance and went screaming to a neighbor.

"It's a bill! Read it! What's it for? I can't pay a bill!"

With difficulty she made herself heard over the din.

"You idiot! It's a check." Then knowing my fondness for buying Christmas presents at any odd time money fell into my hands, she took me firmly by the shoulders and said, "And you're going to buy something for yourself if I have to put a ring in your nose."

So, with a great sense of purpose, I set out to shop for the first "wardrobe" I had ever bought in my life. The shopping center was gay with autumn. I wandered in a confused fog of bright color. Pant suits unlimited didn't tempt me at all; I knew I would look like a well-stuffed sausage in those. Suave suits and soft crepes; flowers, stripes, solids and checks; I lifted one after another from the racks and put them back. Suddenly I was faced with a nasty truth about myself. I had absolutely not the foggiest notion of what sort of clothes I preferred, much less what would be appropriate for the occasion, or what would transform this caterpillar into at least some simple butterfly.

Well!

At that moment my eye was caught by something black and wispy across the aisle. It was on a rack of negligees, and it swayed gently in invitation.

I didn't want a negligee.

I walked straight to the rack like a well-trained hound on a scent. We looked at one another. Heaven forfend, it was a black lace caftan. I didn't need it, but I wanted it more than I had ever wanted any superfluous thing in my life. Did I buy it? You'd better believe I did, and a precious good thing it was. For with the black lace over my arm, the spell was broken and I was able to choose a quite modest but adequate wardrobe.

One thing more: as I left the shop, the black lace whispered from its folds of tissue, "Fabric Store." I obeyed, and there I bought the rosy velvet and the deep white silk fringe to make the shawl that has been my banner through lo these many moons and many miles.

Suddenly I was truly a "liberated" woman, free to be my own vain silly self—loving the touch of velvet and lace. Gone were the sturdy brogans, the shapeless caterpillar skin that had done "well enough." It was a sobering thought at that. If I had ever entertained the notion that I was somehow set apart and favored with any trace of grace or wisdom, or was any example of the efficient mother cum author, the breaking of the chrysalis put me firmly in my place. I was no plaster saint but as bubble-headed a female as ever came out of the twenties. And it felt good to have wings. With some last shred of reticence, I showed the lace and velvet to my sons. They whooped in glee.

"I can't believe it, mom! Lace? And velvet? Why?"

I laughed in sudden happiness.

"Why? Because, you see, I'm a girl!"

They regarded me with a new and very flattering wonder.

"You sure are, mom! You're quite a girl!" And that was accolade enough.

There you have it! Writing a book, regardless of what it may mean to anyone else, and regardless of the subject, sooner or later brings writers face to face with themselves. After the months or years of reaching for a phrase, of brief high inspiration, of bouncing from the conviction that they are great geniuses to the fear that they are utter fools, the first real benefit the authors receive from that first book is that at last they stand revealed to themselves. If they fail they know how they will react to failure. If they succeed, they are either pompous or graceful in success. And knowing the truth about themselves, they may graduate in time to seeing with a clearer eye the truth around them.

Because by the mercy of God I was born to be Indian, the subjects most interesting to me would be those that most vitally affected my people, and I would be concerned about those things. But forever and forever, if I wrote, I would write as a woman—accepting the fact, glorying in it. Away with the superfluous arguments as to whether a woman can earn a living, put meat on the table, or shoes on the feet. That was proved by our great-grandmothers in ancient times. Away with the adolescent question of whether she should be eligible for this and that; she has only to reach—with good purpose.

Or whether she be "equal."

Equal? Ha! Was it built into that first grandmother to see that there be not meat alone, but roses upon the table? She provided that extra touch of love or sympathy; that extra radiance that lifted humankind from the staid business of life to add all the loveliness of lace and velvet, roses and white linen to the world of harsh reality.

I settled my new-found wings more comfortably as I flew into the next chapter, and chuckled.

"Thank you, God. I'm a girl."

CHAPTER 3

Journey into Light

There is one very odd thing about life—that enigma with a capital L. You may be entirely sure you know where you're going and what is going to happen when you get there; and as it turns out, neither your route nor your destination will be what you had expected. I'm not thinking about those minor catastrophes that keep popping up to interfere with your plans; though I've learned to be very careful not to say, "There! That problem is solved. The rest is gravy." That's a sure sign something else will befall to slam you into the sidewalk.

Having had some experience, I can deal with problems. The recurring emergencies in raising a houseful of active, imaginative outgoing children taught me one thing: entering an emergency situation is rather like going through a tunnel. If you just keep putting down one foot after another, sooner or later you reach the end of it.

The thing that really leaves me gasping is to start something I believe will be strictly routine and have the heavens open and pour down undreamed-of blessings.

Or to think I know a lot and find that I really know very little—but that what I finally come to learn is far and away much better than I could have imagined.

That's rather involved, so I see that I shall have to begin at the beginning—which is a logical place to start, but not nearly so much fun as to start in the middle.

Well, then, to begin with, for most of my life I had been a moderate sort of Christian. I wasn't really proud of that, incidentally, and if anyone asked me, I would say firmly and with feeling, "Yes, I'm a believer." But my answer would have been tinged with the gentle surprise that might have been followed by, "Isn't everyone?"

Oh, I was convinced that in Jesus we have a dear friend, ever present in times of trouble. At other times, I'm sure, I gave the matter only passing thought. Of one thing I was quite sure; getting up in meeting to "testify" wasn't for me. What an embarrassing thing to do! Why, I had seen strong men weep. No, definitely, my religion was going to be a very private thing. If I had doubts or temptations I'd take them up with God in the privacy of my boudoir.

How was I to know that the time would come when I would "speak out in meeting"—not just to my own small group of friends but in churches large and small in places I had never hoped to see—and that in doing this undreamed-of thing I would be caught up in an ecstasy of gladness and of love? How was I to believe, sitting there in my neat little shell, that when Jesus said, "Fear not; for the words will be prepared for you," he meant exactly what he said, and that that truth was for anyone, even me?

Now I had "flown into the next chapter" and felt that I was prepared for the autograph party sort of thing. A dear friend who writes for our local newspaper and who has several books to her credit had set me straight on a few items.

"It's nothing to worry about, dear," she said, "strictly routine promotion. Just sign your name, and don't get carried away."

Ah, if she could only know what really happened! Strictly routine, indeed!

How merciful it was that I should start on my adventure with a last sweet glimpse of old familiar scenes and people. There is a beautiful park in our area where every variety of shrub or tree that can possibly be coaxed into growing in a temperate zone may be found. Dawes Arboretum is the focal point for many of our community programs. Nature study, bird walks, picnics large and small, classes in bonsai, and weddings in the beautiful Japanese garden—all of these march in gay procession through the summer. In winter it is quiet with that hush of leafless woodlands, but its great trees lift bare arms and wait for the stirring of spring—for the children and the lush carpet of violets and spring beauties. It is most precious to me because on a bluff across the road, the little cemetery holds the grave of Grey Owl, overlooking a peaceful, pine-shaded lake.

The park holds many memories, for my children were often involved there with youth activities. Sometimes the boys were called upon to don feather bustles and dance; sometimes I talked to small groups; and sometimes we simply went to wander the paths, to sit on the warm earth.

At any rate, I had been asked to take part in a "Friendship Day," and it was to be held the very day before I left for Independence. Feeling a touch of impatience when I had so much to do, the house to close, and bags to be packed, I stood at last before that crowd in the assembly hall. I looked—and saw not strangers but my neighbors. Here were the people we had feared those many years ago...the people who had feared us more, perhaps. The first uneasy steps into an alien world had been taken here, and these were the hands stretched forth to help us enter.

I told them this; how it had been to come as strangers to a strange new world, the kindly things they'd done, the ready smiles that set our fears at rest. I hoped that it would always be the same for others as they came. We laughed about old times and marveled that the children I remembered now had families of their own.

It was a lovely, quiet, filling day. Half of the people followed me home; there we kicked off our shoes and put the coffee on. Good conversation flowed—of books, and birds, and schools...and Indians. One teacher grieved because there was so little information available. I laid a stack of folders on the table and said that this was information I received each week from the Bureau of Indian Affairs. She turned her head in anger. She had heard about the BIA and wanted no part of what it had to say.

I laughed, remembering: "Can any good come out of Nazareth?" The folders were reprints from newspapers across the country, accounts of Indian problems and projects, many of them bitterly critical of the agency that dispensed this information. Everyone wants to know about Indians, but the reading of reports is dull business. Tribal income, unemployment, Indians trying to start a supermarket—none of this is as exciting as Indians on horseback around the wagon train (except to other Indians). But that, as my granddaughter would say, is where it's at; and when you get into it, it really is exciting. To see people hauling themselves up by the proverbial bootstraps, beginning once more to stand up in some dignity; to see them reach out to one another across the gap of division and neglect—that's something else! These clippings were the thoughts and dreams of Indians, and at last we agreed that the BIA did indeed "do something."

At last my friends took their leave with warm good wishes—all but one, a woman with many woes and an overwhelming need to share them. She poured them out and I said "Oh?" and "Ah!" and drank the cup of her grief, feeling great tenderness for this old friend, though half her problem is her own self-pity. What of that? Pain, even if it's self-inflicted, is no less pain.

At last, at last I set my bags out on the floor and stowed the contents, hoping against hope the clasps would hold. The buckskins and the caftan and the shawls and other garments, papers, notebooks...all the gear I thought so necessary.

David, my son, looked on in grim amusement. "It's a good thing you're not backpacking," he said.

At the airport the black panic set in once more. I turned to that strong right arm and whispered, "Oh, Dave, I'm scared."

He gave me a little shove and said, "Don't worry, mom, you'll knock 'em dead. You'll lay 'em in the aisles."

That was a bit irreverent, as it turned out, but the right treatment at the moment. These were just the words I'd used for those brief bouts of stage fright before their class plays and their dances.

Then bippety-bop down the landing strip and the earth began to draw back under the wings. The great bird folded its legs with a solemn clop-clop and we shot into a new universe.

Oh, lovely sky-land, full of popcorn balls and sugar candy! Here and there great shapes arose...Neptune riding a dolphin? What at first I thought to be a Grecian lady with a high coiffure turned out to be Davy Crocket in a coonskin cap. And far away along the horizon, flat-topped cloudshapes like icebergs on a sea of blue. Oh, lovely sky-land!

"The heavens declare the glory of the Lord!" sang my heart. The works of humankind had faded into nothingness. The concrete, the smoke and noise, the junk piles... all had disappeared. The heavens *declare*—affirm, insist the glory of God. Down then we dropped like a leaf falling—through the cloudgates, and there she lay, dear Mother Earth serene and patient. Though she had been laced down with roads and fences, her rivers corraled, a stone burden laid at will, still with love she opened her arms to receive us.

And there were the two dear friends to meet me, to whisk me out of this awesome terminal (hideous word) and take me to a place of peace and beauty. Did they sense my panic? Everything translates into Indian for me, it seems. What was I doing here, a "dumb Indian," a pretender at wisdom?

Here in this house of peace was a woman who was all that we mean when we say "Christian." This lovely, unpretentious, orderly house; this lovely unpretentious, ordered life! I looked about and hoped the Master when he comes might come here first to rest and to refresh himself after his journey from his Father's kingdom. I sat enthralled, hearing the tale of how she and her husband built a church in Alaska, going out each morning to sweep the snow from the golden logs... blue eyes twinkling, alive with faith, accepting loss and disappointment in perfect trust.

There were soft strains of music as she played the hymns we would sing at a service... a stack of bright cottons for clothes for a grandchild. This was the disciplined peace against which I had spent my life rebelling. And yet—through those nights I spent in the house of my sister in Christ—an insistent idea was beginning to stir in my mind. There was a familiar feeling in this house. Where had I known this quiet peace, this utter partnership with God? I had heard all the sermons about Christian homes, stewardship, increase of blessings. Here I saw the evidence, the epitome of the ideal. But—there was something more here, some...some lovely spirit. Trust? Faith? Security in the love of the Father? Light began to dawn.

Was it possible?

I had known this atmosphere before in a tarpapered shack far to the north, with the rich Oneida voices singing: "Ye-sos, Ye-sos..." the same love, the same peace and trust.

Nothing could have presented such a contrast in its physical aspect as this comfortable modern home and that rough, poorly furnished cabin. Yet this same spirit, this *presence,* permeated both.

Oh, merciful God, was it possible?

With the slow awakening of my people there was a stirring of bitterness, of rejection of all that was not Indian. Divisions between Christian Indians and those who wanted to follow the old ways of the people had arisen so that we were very careful not to talk about religion. It was a beautiful thing to be a Christian, a beautiful thing to be Indian. There were these vague, uneasy suspicions that one could not be both and do them well.

Was it possible that our bark, drifting through the dark centuries, had come so close to this bright shore without our knowing it? My mind accepted the evidence of where my people had been in the past, of the mighty truths our fathers knew in that dim day beyond the legends.

My heart knew that in the fullness of time....
Was the time closer than I had dreamed?

The days were filled with new adventures. We went to the publishing house to meet the team that had made my book a reality; to chat with editors and secretaries, artists, and all the busy crew. Back into the printing rooms where giant presses hummed, I saw white pages falling down, moving along to drop at last all folded and delivered precisely in the place where they belonged. What magic! This, then, was the "mysterious thing" publishers did with a book. All these people doing this and that, and great machines and cameras and typewriters and printers and errand runners—and a book!

So you might say I came to the "strictly routine" part of the trip with some preparation. Nothing prepared me—or could have—for the rush of love when I sat at the table to sign books for people I had never met before. Not strangers these—we had a bond! I had written a book, with a lot of help, of course; they had read the book, or at least were willing to read it. They came smiling, to chat about families, to affirm their faith, and there was nothing "strictly routine" about it.

Nothing could have prepared me for finding that young Omaha brother who came to act as escort while I signed the books. What inborn, natural courtesy my people have! There was a time when I would not have moved without a "warrior escort" at my side, but that was long ago. Yet here he was, noble of face and form; a youth who had known great pain, yet who walked so proudly. Oh, Omaha, take heart; with sons like these, how can the ancient tree be fallen?

Such a pitch of high excitement as we knew that week! Visits to churches 'round about to witness, but to receive much more of truth and love than I had to give.

Potluck banquets where my careful diet crashed, TV programs, schools, and guests. Just once did I come back to earth, to sit soaking up my own identity within the Kansas City Urban Indian Center. Here were the hardworking, sweat-shirted, denimed young Indians who daily face the problems of their people: where to find a job, a place to live, financial aid for school, help for the alcoholic. We sat around the table and we talked—and talked—and talked—of hope, frustration, legislation, and brave new dreams. We marveled that short years ago, the nations represented here could not have met within a mile, and here they were, all working hard and quite delighted with each other. We reached to touch each other in that newly wakened spirit of old brotherhood. There was a feeling very close to tears to realize that, after all the dead, we few were here, but very much alive.

And so at last I found myself ensconced behind that lectern in a church that holds so much of the history of my faith. A few brief prayers and then the music bore me to that strange, new place. My heart was very still—waiting, but for what? And the words came—and with them a new knowledge, a new awareness so that the weakness in my faith stood out in bold relief. As I talked about the ancient history of my people, I had the eerie experience of a series of flashbacks and thought, "It really does happen." I heard Grey Owl's words, "Not until you enter the waters of baptism and receive the gift of the Holy Spirit can you even begin to understand the truth of Christ," and felt again a quick resentment at that implied criticism.

I had been the vessel into which Grey Owl had poured his memories, his faith, and his love for his people. The years of searching old books and records for the dim footprints of the ancients had been full of excitement;

but the mechanics of financing those years of research and of getting the book ready for publication had dimmed the impact of its message for the writer. Even my baptism, joyful and spiritually uplifting as it had been, had not turned the final key to lock me into the full awareness of Christ.

I was committed, but with the inherent defensive attitude that plagued my people through much of their experience with Christian doctrine—and, I suspect, many others who recognized the social impact of his message, but who could not go the final mile.

I thought of all the wars fought in his name, of all the voices calling, "Come this way"..."No, that." Confusion. Victims caught in the Inquisition, the rape of the southland for its gold, the burning of books—in the name of Christ. And in my secret heart I had had some reservations about this Jesus, whose work had brought such sorry things to pass.

I had been blaming Christ for the deeds of human beings who may be misguided, or evil, or enchanted with their own power, but surely not my Lord, who left the glories of his Father's kingdom to bring the precious message of God's love to all the lost, forgotten sheep across the world.

I would never, never again be able to sit complacent in the face of evil. If I really believed the words that I was speaking, that our Creator had given to humankind the stewardship of earth and the agency to choose to follow good or evil, then if through indolence or unconcern I tolerate the increase of evil on this holy earth for which my Savior died—dear God, be merciful, I would be guilty by compliance.

Then in one blinding thunderbolt of insight, I joined the ageless throng who down the corridors of time have hoped and dreamed and died for love of the Lord of the

Dawn. The mighty truth was greater than the pain.
*The heavens declare—
All earth awaits the coming of her King.*

CHAPTER 4

The Culture

It was a college-level class in Minorities Studies, and the film being shown opened with a shot of a low concrete building. The unpaved parking area showed a predominance of pickup trucks, most of which displayed evidence of dusty travels. The cameras were moved inside the building where some two hundred pairs of busy hands moved expertly over intricate electronic assembly. Other workers moved about picking up finished products, delivering an assortment of gadgetry which ultimately would emerge as circuits.

The amazing thing was that for all the complexity of capacitors, transistors, and diodes, the workers used no schematics, no charts or diagrams. The eyes saw the pattern of wires and components and fitted this to that as a matter of course. These were the same hands that could weave a rug design in precise detail without a pattern. Mind conceived, transmitted to hands, and the pattern emerged. These were Navajo, quiet, and very talented.

The plant supervisor, as Indian as his staff, traced the history and format of the plant. Words like profit-sharing, work force, self-help, and fringe benefits fell naturally from his lips.

Three hundred people out of a population of several hundred thousand is perhaps not a very impressive figure; but this sampling of Indian industry, self-help, and skill had been designed to illustrate Indian culture, twentieth century style. The film ended, and the professor shook his head.

"Personally, I find that very sad," he said. "A beautiful culture lost forever."

There was a war-whoop from the back of the room. The professor had one Indian in his class. The young man leaped to his feet and poured forth a tirade of long-suppressed resentment.

"Lost their culture!" he stormed, the words tumbling over each other. "What in the name of all that's holy do you think Indian culture was about? To sit in the dirt and starve? To stand in a welfare line? To beg for favors from the Great White Father? Here are three hundred families whose children are fed and clothed—by their parent's efforts—*that's* Indian culture. Three hundred people using their natural skill to master a new art!"

He stalked to the door and turned.

"I quit this class. Any man who could hold a doctorate and know so little is no fit teacher for me or my kind."

This savage resentment about the popular definition of culture is increasing among Indians. Here are some other comments.

A young attorney: Out of a background of intense poverty and the apathy it often spawns, he spent four years in the Marine Corps and, on his VA educational grant, went on to win his stripes in law at one of the most demanding of schools.

"You see," he says, "we were told to get education,

learn the white man's ways, and succeed in business or the professions. But if we show evidence that we have acquired the expertise to, for instance, manage a police force, set up courts, right away someone starts complaining that we have too much sovereignty. If we learn to manage our resources and out of them provide a decent standard of living for our people, we get this nonsense about losing our culture. 'They' would still rather have us in tepees."

Another: The tourists stood watching as the silversmith put the finishing touches on a bracelet of elegant design. Its matching necklace was spread on the scarred table—and the customer for whom the set was designed stood by with his check for twelve hundred dollars.

In the silent crowd one man stood somberly, sadly shaking his head (like the professor). At last the Indian raised his eyes from his work and addressed the tourist with a cold curiosity. "Stranger," he said, "why are you sad?"

"Well, Chief," replied the tourist, "there is no doubt that you are a great artist, but it does make me sad to see you commercializing your art."

The Indian exploded into anger.

"Why is it," he demanded, "that when your people make something and sell it, it's business. When we make something and sell it, we're commercializing our art or losing our culture? And furthermore..." here the hammer descended on the table causing an assortment of equipment and supplies to leap like exclamation points, "furthermore, don't call me Chief!"

Then there was the classic response from a young Indian who, when asked why he did not dress in the beautiful garments of his ancestors, queried, "From which period?"

To our people who, indeed, have great love and respect for ancestors and for their way of life, this insistence on the tepee and tomahawk image is ignorant—and insulting. It makes no more sense than to say that Blacks should pick cotton and filch watermelons, or that English people should not be seen without a suit of armor, or a Scot without his kilt. And perish the thought that any American should cook on an electric stove, abandoning that foundation of the culture, the woodpile.

Are there no Indians who live as they used to live? Yes, of course—on a limited scale. There are Indians in out-of-the-way places where adobe brick is still the most efficient and the most readily obtainable material for their homes...where it is still practical, and much more comfortable, to bake bread in an outside oven.

To say that it is "enriching" to haul water twenty or thirty miles, or even that it is traditional is a flagrant misunderstanding of the real "ancient culture." When we go back to our roots we find that our ancestors would simply have transferred the village to the water, in the course of which they sometimes had to do battle with those already in possession of it. Who wants to move over...or out? How many thousands of square miles of territory would have to be relinquished so that one or two million people might support themselves by the buffalo hunt?

Of course, it's nonsense—but so is the attitude which is the logical extreme of this pattern of thought (and in case you might think that the following experience is an exaggeration, let me assure you that it is not unusual).

The woman came into my tiny shop and pawed restlessly through the display of beadwork, so carefully fashioned and at such cost to the eyesight.

"Oh, yes," she said, "We saw all this junk down at Cherokee, North Carolina."

I had never been to Cherokee, though I longed to go, so I was interested to hear her account of the restored village and the people who lived and worked there.

"I'll never set foot in that place again," she continued, "I have never in my life been so insulted."

It took very little urging for the story to come out.

"No, I didn't go to the village; that's all a fake...they don't really live there. And no, I didn't see the pageant; I'm not interested in that. I wanted to see how they really lived. There was this old man who had a little stand along the road, selling stuff like what you have here. I asked him where he lived and he just pointed up the mountain. 'Can I go up there and see your house?' I asked, and he looked me square in the eye and just said no."

I should have let it go at that, but I had to try. "What does your husband do?" I asked.

"He has a hardware business," she answered.

"Tell me...what do you think he would say if a total stranger walked in and said she wanted to go and see where and how he lived?"

"That's entirely different," the woman answered.

In all fairness, this account must be followed by an episode which involved a neighbor who, not surprisingly, has become my dearest friend. She and her family had spent a month touring in "Indian country" and had come home tanned and refreshed. She told me about the high points.

"One place we stopped, there was a woman weaving a beautiful rug on one of those primitive upright looms. Well, you know, I'm a weaver, myself, though nothing like that...and once I start to weave, I don't want anyone to breathe! But I sat down where I wouldn't be in the way and just watched. And do you know, that loom made sense! I could see how efficient it really was, with the pattern growing inch by inch. I could have sat there all day, but the most precious thing was that after a while she looked up and said, 'How about a cup of coffee?' We had such a nice visit and," she added happily, "I'm going back next summer and take some of my weaving to show her."

Let's look at this culture business to see whether Indians are really losing touch or whether they can maintain the elements which made the ancient ways satisfying and good.

First and foremost, implicit in all Indian culture was the reverence for the Creator's gifts brought forth from Mother Earth, and for his aids in the process—sun and rain. Fail to experience this truth, and we fail step one in Indian culture. The fact that Indians today still maintain this concept of the Creator who is ever-active in the manifestations of his creative spirit, *and our obligation of stewardship* over those gifts, is one piece of evidence that Indian culture is far from "dead." To fully express this concept, however, will require the spreading of this gospel to white neighbors. There are tribes today beneath whose lands are resources worth millions of dollars. The people are poor, and those resources would solve many of their problems; but they are going to hold up those contracts until they can find a way to develop those resources without damage to their lands—and until the contract bids are commensurate with those offered to other citizens. In spite of our increased concern with ecology, this attitude is frowned on by developers more concerned with profits than with conservation.

In Indian culture, each child was loved and cared for by many relatives, equally responsible with his or her parents. The child was introduced by close association to the manners, mores, and responsibilities of adults. There was no room for lazy people, or those who would lie comatose with drink while others performed their share of the labor. Those people, male or female, would simply have starved—and good riddance. Sociologists have made much of the fact that there was no social stigma attached to alcohol—true, no social stigma for the act, but quite possibly a very empty stomach. Each individual's own expectation was not only that he or she would be able to take care of his or her own, but of others as well.

No hunter of any competence or self-respect would have taken meat until the old, the infirm were supplied—all the movies notwithstanding. Most tribes had standard rules covering the division of meat; often the first cut went to the wife's mother. These firm social rules and customs were not learned in ten easy lessons but were absorbed from earliest childhood.

Here we run into a spot of trouble.

First, children. "Indian culture" without the children is inconceivable. They are the listeners to the histories, the legends and traditions, and they will be the tellers of tales to later generations, ad infinitum. They are the ultimate incentive to do a little better, to be a little wiser; and if all other considerations fail, Indians love their children.

Whether Indians may retain this very essential facet of culture depends on a number of conditions over which, at least until recently, they have had no control.

Meet Charlie and Bertha Onefeather (not their names) and the Reverend and Mrs. Blank. When the Reverend Blank was assigned to Charlie's reservation he began his duties with zeal as well as with a deepening horror as he became more intimately acquainted with the prevailing poverty abounding in the region. Charlie and Bertha were as poor as most, and no poorer than many, but they had one treasure—one "little ewe lamb," a child of such sunny disposition and charm that she was a joy to all. The Blanks were no exception. They bought her a doll, singled out the prettiest clothes passed on from a generous congregation, and begged for the privilege of having her pass a night or so in their home. The parents were flattered and grateful, for they could not provide these extra benefits on their limited income. Besides, was it not an accepted custom that both the joy and the care of children should be shared?

Over the following year the love of the Blanks for the child, and the trust of the parents in their child's benefactors, grew into a fine friendship. Then fate, in the person of the Mission Board, stepped in. The Blanks were called to serve in other fields. A tearful Mrs. Blank approached the parents.

"We are so sad at leaving this child who has become like a daughter to us. Let her come with us, just for a little while; just for the winter so she will be warm and can go to school."

Charlie and Bertha thought about what their lives would be without this happy child, but they thought, too, of the approaching cold, the inevitable separation if the child went to a boarding school, the only alternative. In short, they capitulated with a reluctant sense of gratitude.

And that was the last they saw of their daughter!

There were no letters. The Blanks disappeared. Subsequent missionaries either could not or would not reveal their whereabouts. Spring came, but not the child. Had she died and their friends were afraid to tell the parents? Finally, Charlie and Bertha sold their few possessions, the neighbors contributed what they could, and the couple loaded a few necessitites into the ancient truck. If you see them at a camp meeting or a revival, do not ask them if they have found their child, for they have not. But they are still looking.

An extreme case? Not at all. Thousands of Indian children have been separated from their culture by just such "well-meaning" Christian people who have not—whether they are lay people or of the cloth—caught the first inkling of what Christian love is all about.

There is, too, the matter of law. Laws regarding the placement of children are geared to the dominant society. The standards under the law for "adequate" housing and income make it impossible for Indian foster parents to qualify in cases of emergency or permanent child Care. "Preservation of culture" has had no place in the law, nor is the ancient "extended family system" recognized. Children have been removed without the consent of relatives for such nebulous reasons as "they will be better off," or "the Reservation is not a fit environment."

In an attempt to stem the tide of the loss of their children, tribal governments have begun to enact ordinances governing the removal or placement of Indian children. Some states, also, now have laws forbidding the removal of children outside state boundaries or general culture areas. But until we have informed courts, informed Indian parents, or until we reach that utopia where the worth of persons is the primary consideration, this immoral abuse will continue in some degree.

The map showing the various "culture areas" is familiar to most Americans. One could hardly pass through eight years of school or progress far in the Boy Scouts without at least viewing it in passing. The areas are designated as Northeastern Woodland, Southeastern Woodland, Northern Plains, Southwestern and Northwest Coast.

Anyone who is interested may find countless books—and many of them very good books—describing in rich detail the varying customs of the people who inhabited these regions *at the moment of first contact* with incoming settlers. The dates of these first contacts are also varied.

Consider the noble Lenni Lenape, once known among their neighbors as "Grandfathers," a title of the highest respect. In 1609—when English navigator Henry Hudson, employed by the Dutch East India Company, explored what is now Delaware Bay—the Lenni Lenape occupied territory at its northern extremity, New Jersey, Pennsylvania, and southeastern New York. A year later Captain Samuel Argall, an English sailor from Virginia, sailed to the entrance of the bay and named the cape at its mouth after the Governor of Virginia, Lord de la Warr. Altered to Delaware, the name became attached to the western borders along the bay. The Lenni Lenape thus became popularly known as Delaware's Indians.

It was not until 1682 that William Penn made his famous "Walking Purchase" treaty, and it was not until 1867 that the nucleus of this once numerous people was settled on Cherokee lands in Oklahoma. During those 165 years as they were forced westward, they settled successively in such diversified territories as western Pennsylvania, Ohio, Indiana, Missouri, Arkansas, Kansas, and Texas. Few, if any, of the materials implicit to their culture on the eastern seaboard would have been found in Texas, certainly...and few in their final destination. Change in the original mode of life was inevitable as new materials became available.

Materially, the culture pattern was altered. The soul of the Lenni Lenape remained intact; and in a very strange, long-unrecognized way. Through the seventeenth and eighteenth centuries the great majority of Delawares were converted to the Christian faith. With all due respect to David Zeisberger, the Moravian missionary who endured the harsh conditions of wilderness life to introduce the gospel, the conversions took place largely because the Lenni Lenape found within the scriptures laws, customs, and beliefs entirely compatible with their own religion.

We move into the Plains and become enmeshed in the culture of the Sioux, the ancient Lakota. We find them throughout the Dakotas, eastern Montana and northern Nebraska. We see great horsemen, warriors, hunters of buffalo, tepees glowing in the night fires—surely here is the "real culture" we are looking for.

The Sioux were not on the Plains until 1640. Prior to that comparatively recent date they were Woodland Indians with all that the name implies.

According to accounts of the early French explorers the Sioux had moved north to the headwaters of the Mississippi during the late sixteenth and early seventeenth centuries. Few historians have speculated from just how far south they had come. If we were to follow tradition, we would trace them very far south indeed. They may well have shared with many other northern tribes a Central American origin which would certainly upset all our ideas of Indian culture.

At any rate, as late as 1640 they were Woodland people, building wigwams of bark and hide, expert canoemen on the white waters. It was, in fact, not until 1851 that they ceded to the United States the last of their territory east of the Mississippi. Buffalo were found in some numbers in the East; the extensive concentration of herds was on the plains. But it was the horse, apparently, on which the Lakota rode into history as the ideal in Indian culture—a very late, and brief, segment of the long history of this great and adaptable people.

It is, in fact, that very word "adaptable"—so long ignored—that best defines what Indian culture was all about. The tribe is hardly to be found that does not hold in the archives of its legends memories of other climes, ancient ancestors "who lived a different life...and were very wise"—wise enough, and with skill enough, to accept and adopt such materials as were to be found in new locations. Where there was good clay and little else, they produced pottery of superior form and design. Where other materials were predominant, the art of the potter declined and new skills grew.

Thus we see that the whole concept of Indian culture is very nebulous indeed—unless, of course, we recognize it as it should be, the expression of the heart and soul of a people bent on survival and on the development of a good and satisfying life-style.

The Navajo at his computer, going home each weekend to cut his mother's supply of wood, to move her sheep from the summer to the winter range, is entirely in keeping with tradition. He is simply a hunter after new game.

The urban Indian, scouting for new skills, new working materials for his people, is as much a part of true culture as was his grandfather blazing a trail.

Look at them. Look and do not grieve; for they ride out and away from the sunset of extinction into a new phase of culture. This people, whose cornfields extended for such miles of territory that a whole regiment armed with torches could not destroy them, though they tried...this people, whose ancestors built irrigation systems and raised earthworks in an excess of energy and zeal are in no danger of "losing their culture"—unless, of course, the last breath is stilled, the last heart stops beating, and the last Indian eye is closed.

CHAPTER 5

On Identity

This is not a "comfortable" subject, but it is one which must be faced. The establishment and recognition of the identity of Indians may, or may not, be very important to you, but if there is going to be any communication it is equally important that you know what they mean by the word.

Indians have always had complaints about their situation; but it was the coinage of the word *identity* that enabled them to pinpoint the real difficulty.

"That's what's wrong," they began to say. "We have lost our identity. 'They' have taken our identity."

Hearing this plaint many well-meaning people ask in some confusion, "What on earth do they mean by *identity?* Here we're all Americans; we don't need any other identity."

Then there are people—Indians call them "tourist types"—who are quite sure they know what is meant.

"Indians don't want to hold a job or live as we do. They want to go back to the tepee and the hunt."

It must be traumatic to see their subject snarl and show its teeth. How do we get hold of this slippery word *identity?* To attempt to define it and its importance is a little like trying to explain a Christmas tree. A tree is beautiful without any extra adornment if seen in the forest. To be a Christmas tree, it has to have trimmings, and they have to be the particular trimmings that awaken memories of other Yuletides: the glass parasol Aunt Emma brought from Paris a generation ago, the Santa Claus with its colors dimmed and chipped, icicles placed with care or flung by the handful (according to family custom), swaths of tinsel or cranberry strings—to each his own. I have known friends who invested great sums in a pure white artificial tree and blue lights, only to revert later to a more traditional expression of Christmas cheer.

To the Indian, however, the loss of identity is all this—and more. It represents all the values once lived by: language, religion, the extended family, and the clan system, at once the Indian's security blanket and genetic health.

To lose one's identity is to have no base from which to build. It is, of course, idle to speculate on what might have happened if Columbus had missed his mark. Once there were mighty empires in the Americas with trade routes, communication, education, retirement benefits, a ruling class, and formal religion. Would their influence in time have extended to all the corners of this land as had apparently begun to happen?

Would the warring tribes eventually have remembered their brotherhood and concentrated on establishing a united nation? Would the invitation of the Iroquois Confederacy for all those who so desired to assemble under the tree of peace have meant more time for agriculture and the building of towns? Given an extra hundred years or so, the nations might have presented a far different reception...and might even have placed a higher monetary value on Manhattan.

True—it's an idle speculation. They did not have that extra hundred years to recuperate after the generations of warfare and to begin to experience that growth which comes to a settled population. The European peoples entering the country had had many centuries of slow growth influenced by many cultures between the ancient days of tribal wanderers and their own particular brand of civilization. The mindless thrust of ambition forced the Indian of that period into much the same position as a sixth-grade child being promoted into college and expected to earn a degree. It stopped the natural evolution of Indian culture dead in its tracks and exposed a gap between the old and newer concept of society that still troubles Indians of today.

In the aftermath of the westward expansion, and in the popular belief in manifest destiny, the Indian was squeezed into smaller and smaller boundaries until there was no way the familiar pattern of life could be maintained.

The question has been asked: "Why could they not maintain themselves on the reservation as they did before? That's why they were put there in the first place."

The question and the following statement display a singular lack of knowledge of ecology and of history. There is simply no way to relate the hunt engaged in for sport or recreation to the socioeconomic basis hunting and gathering provided in that period of Indian history. Those who are now engaged in wildlife management know that great areas are essential to maintain even a moderate population of game. Deer, bear, elk, and buffalo must constantly move about for forage and to allow the area they have grazed to renew itself. Even if the buffalo had not been slaughtered almost to extinction, they would not have been available in constant supply on those fragments of territory.

The skills that the Indians had learned over long generations were part of their pride, for they provided the self-assurance that they were adequate to the task of contributing to the well-being of their families and communities. It was, therefore, only common sense that a clause be inserted in the treaties defining the responsibility of the government to provide "rations" until such time as the Indians could establish an economy on some other basis. And just in case the government might fail to do this, the wise old chiefs insisted on the insertion of a clause ensuring their descendants the right to hunt and fish in their former hunting grounds.

As it turned out, these issues became the supreme tragedy for the people they were to serve...and the shame of the people who promised them. The files of records of the War Department and later of the Bureau of Indian Affairs fill many shelves in the Department of the Interior and the Library of Congress. They are rife with accounts of shipments of goods and tools allocated but never delivered, of Indians petitioning to go on a hunt or pleading to be allowed to present their plight to the "white father in Washington," of bacon and flour stored in warehouses until they were rancid and infested, of this spoiled food being released to the Indian to make room for fresh supplies. This is a matter of public record, and although there is not much we can do about it now, it gives a first glimpse of the tragic loss of identity in a formerly self-sustaining people.

The once proud father standing in line for spoiled rations, the industrious mother who once knew exactly what to do with the gifts of the land, now sitting in ragged despair on the steps of the agent's office—these were the tragic "first wave" of social and economic changes.

It soon became apparent that something would have to be done. Even in the aftermath of war, there were people who felt some sympathy or admiration for Indians, though their methods were often ill-considered. In 1819 Congress appropriated $10,000 to initiate programs for the "civilization of Indians." The money was funneled through the War Department to the newly emerging Bureau of Indian Affairs which had no capability to institute a program of education. Consequently, the task was subcontracted and funds appropriated to various religious groups. Their zeal was directed not so much to education as to making Christian converts—each to its own particular doctrine. It was policy from the beginning to completely sever a child from its environment and with anything that might contribute to a fond memory of or a pride in that environment. This policy is set forth in early reports, not just as a part of the record but with a glow of self-satisfaction on the part of administrators.

During the next hundred years, the school system sank into a cloud of invisibility. Except for the copious reports passing through authorized channels, the public was totally uninformed—and possibly largely disinterested. The official consensus of opinion was that Indian children were inherently inferior and all that could be done was to "Americanize" them as much as possible. This meant banning their language, cutting their hair, and forcing them to abhor anything that had to do with the cultural folkways.

In 1928, however, the Meriam Commission report provided a shocking evaluation of Indian boarding schools, some run by religious groups and others by government agencies. Often the schools were housed in abandoned military installations. The report confirmed rumors of severe corporal punishment and even of brutality and sexual abuse. The two misdemeanors most likely to call for punishment were speaking a native language and running off to go home.

In 1934, with the passage of the Johnson-O'Malley bill, local public schools received appropriations with the hope that they would have the incentive not only to enroll Indian children but to provide programs which would help them cope with their specific needs. This plan was not immediately successful due to a lack of qualified teachers who fully understood the needs of Indian children. In-depth studies and the development of special programs lay in the future. Consequently, there were complaints of the funds being used for other programs. The main difficulty, however, lay in the fact that the children who most urgently needed this help came from isolated areas where there were no public schools. Often they were taken from their homes to be placed in BIA operated dormitories, attending public schools but separated entirely from the local community. Here their native language was still forbidden, and the concept that they were "wards" of the government was ground in repeatedly.

The report in 1971 of the National Association for the Advancement of Colored People, and the six-volume report on Indian Education by Robert Kennedy (*Indian Education, A National Tragedy—A National Challenge*) revealed the fact that the primary accomplishment of the system was to convince the children they were inheritors of a vile tradition that must somehow be purged.

Now, in this "fullness of time," it would seem a sort of miracle that Indians retained even a shred of memory of what was a proud identity. The emerging trends show that not only did they achieve the preservation of old traditions, but they had the strength and will to begin to rebuild their original character.

Let it be emphasized that for the most part when Indians say they want to return to the ways of their fathers, they do not mean going back to a hunting-gathering economy. There are some who have done just that—to see if it can be done, or in the belief that inherent values can in this setting be reestablished. Primarily it is the old values they seek. It is often said that "the Indian had a special feeling for the earth," without analyzing what that feeling was. Indians did not just "love" the earth, exulting in its beauties; they lived and breathed with nature, accepting the turn of the seasons, at one with the grass and the trees, the rocks, and their brothers and sisters of earth and air. I very much doubt that we have any words in the English language to define the particular relationship between Indians and their environment. Harmony, balance, ecology, symbiosis—these are terms we understand in relation to music, the dance, or biology. To Indians they relate to the spiritual nature of creation and people's relation to it.

Indians believe they were given customs, rituals, and cultural skills that expressed this interrelation and which were very much a part of their identity as the Red Children of Earth and Sky. An Indian potter fashioning a bowl is not just making an item of utility, though that is the result. He or she is participating in the life of that clay. The clay does not just yield to the potter's hands; it expresses its own nature in the symmetry of its emerging form.

We might consequently expect to see, as a manifestation of the search for identity, a revived interest in cultural crafts, in old skills. And so it is. Every Urban Indian Center has its regular crafts session; happy, fulfilling hours of rich, shared laughter, busy hands. In Indian social clubs, classes in community-run Indian schools, in a kitchen on a reservation, or around a TV set in Washington, Indians know once again the sweet accomplishments of traditional skills.

It may also be expected that this search will include a desire to return to an ancient religion whose tenets sustained the ancestors through centuries before the white man came. There are various Indian religions, from the Midewi of the Algonquin to the Sun Dance of the Sioux. One of the criticisms Indians were wont to level against the Christian church was that there were so many doctrines. In modern times, however, as Native Americans have come into closer relationship with those of other tribes, it becomes clear that there were many doctrines expressed by different rituals, variations on a theme. Be that as it may, all of these traditional religions stressed the strictest moral ethic, the highest moral values.

I was deeply honored during my visit to the St. Regis Mohawk reservation in New York to receive an invitation to a dance at the Longhouse. It is almost unknown for a Christian to be received into that highly traditional circle. As the small drums began, a chorus of teenage voices broke into old songs I would have thought long passed from memory. With one accord, fifty or sixty young people walked decorously to take their places in the line. There were no wallflowers. Dancing singly or hands linked in couples, they followed one another, weaving a charmed circle of the oneness of the people. There was no whistling, jostling, or horseplay; there was also no doubt that they were having a good time.

When each dance was finished, they returned quietly to their seats as an older man rose and spoke at length in their own language. Not a whisper, not a foot shuffling disturbed his discourse. At its close, there was a chorus of "A-hoh!" and the drums began again.

I asked my young escort how he had learned all those old songs. He answered, "When I was a little boy" (he was then fifteen) "I used to sit on the bench with the singers. I just listened to my elders."

My heart overflowed that night with love for my people and their ways. I have found great joy in a wider vision of Christianity as it should be than I would have dreamed possible, and I long for my people to share that joy—but my spirit is lifted by the Traditionalists and their reverence, their strength of faith, and their concern for one another. Our Lord, I think, would have felt quite at home with them.

In the state of Maryland and overlapping into Virginia, the Piscataway were thought to be extinct for two centuries. They are making a vigorous comeback. Still unrecognized as a tribal entity by the Federal Government, they incorporated under the laws of Maryland as a nonprofit organization, and in less than two years grew to eight hundred members. Strangely, though they were assumed to be extinct, they were converted to Christianity by one of the early Jesuits, Father Andrew White, and are today to be found in the fold of the Roman Catholic church.

The answer to this riddle lies in the reluctance of authorities to place the word "Indian" on a birth certificate. Most Indian parents have this difficulty if they avail themselves of hospitals outside the reservation area. No two of my children's birth certificates match. Some describe both parents as Indian; some the father is white, the mother Indian—or vice versa. On two of them, both parents are listed as white. When we protested, the hospital personnel said, "What's the difference? You could pass for white."

Just what is it going to mean—this hunger for a return to a national identity? With Indians in all the professions, involved in housing programs, business—what do they mean to do anyhow? Leaders and individuals are becoming more vocal, and many expressions of specific goals are being made. William (Redwing) Tayac will, at the death of his aged father, become the twenty-eighth sagamore of the Piscataways, a line that extends back to a period before Columbus. These are his words:

> Traditionalism is the salvation of Indian people. We've taken people who didn't have any tribal identity, who knew they weren't black and they weren't white, knew only they were different, and reinstilled in them pride and a culture. Don't misunderstand. We can't live in the woods anymore. We want to come into the mainstream. We need jobs. We want our people to get their pizza Saturday night and have color TV sets, the children educated, but we don't want them to lose their identity, culture and traditions.*

There remains, then, the supreme test of just how far Indians may go in reaffirming their identity. This test is the recognition of them as they consider themselves, nations of people. "Nations within a Nation" is the popular term and to the people claiming this identity, there seems no conflict between their acting within the law of the land as a whole and being sovereign administrators of their own territories.

Other people have other ideas, of course. A great many persons of goodwill are quite interested in seeing Indians return to their culture, engage in their crafts, perform their dances, even practice their religion, but when it comes down to the nitty-gritty of identity as a separate people—this is where friendship ceases.

One reason for this reluctance may be that most have

---

* Article by Henry Scarupa, the *Sun Magazine*, January 11, 1976.

been programmed to think of "nation" and "conquest" in the same context. The idea, proclaimed by so many orators, that this country has never fought a war of conquest is questionable. In fact, this statement is the height of comedy to Indians, and from where they stand, this reaction is understandable.

Regardless of the outcome of the battles that plague the courts, Indians will probably continue to distinguish between bands as small local entities, tribes as entities comprising several clans, and nations as the overall identity of the related tribes or settlements. It is the official position of this identification which becomes a difficult pill for some people to swallow. It comes as a shock to them to find that many of the tribes have their own flags, their own seals. The fact that Old Glory flies proudly and in its proper place, or that statistics show that Indians have provided an impressive ratio of voluntary enlistments in all their country's wars is often lost sight of.

The solution to this controversy involves much more than "making the Indian happy." It involves the integrity of the American people and the validity of the United States Constitution.

One of the most controversial issues has been Indian fishing rights on the Columbia River, in Puget Sound, and in northwestern Washington. In 1974 U.S. District Judge George H. Boldt ruled that the 1855 Point Elliot treaty was "the law of the land" and that those tribes involved did have the right to half the area's commercial fish catch. The decision unleashed a storm of protest from commercial fishing interests, citizen and recreation interests, and the Fish and Wildlife Commissions.

Though the scream of anguish has echoed and re-echoed down congressional corridors, there has seemed little likelihood that the decision will be reversed. Representative Lloyd Meeds (Democrat, Washington) pointed out that even if Congress would agree to rewrite or junk the treaties, constitutional law requires Indian compensation. That would equal $21 million a year for at least the next century—and possibly the same amount for the time since 1855 when the Washington State treaties were drafted. It would be cheaper, he said, to spend the estimated $200 million investment needed to quadruple fish runs in the Northwest. Needless to say, this statement did not add to his popularity.

Morris Thompson, then U.S. Commissioner of Indian Affairs, addressing the Portland City Club in November 1975, attempted to explain the unique relationship Indian tribes have with the federal government. He said, "This relationship is based on the treaties the United States signed with the tribes as governing bodies, and as coequal governments."

"Thus the relationship is political and not racial," the commissioner added. "The relationship is not based on the fact that the Indian tribes now are a minority in society, nor that they are an ethnically different society, or that they are poor, or that they are red."

The basis for this relationship is specified in the commerce clause of the Constitution in which Congress is charged with the responsibility "to regulate commerce with foreign nations and among the several states and with the Indian tribes." To seal this arrangement and to ensure the ability of Congress to perform these functions, the Constitution provides that "all treaties shall be the supreme law of the land, anything in the Constitution or laws of any state to the contrary notwithstanding."

Since the particular clause in question deals with tribes in the same context as foreign nations, the assumption might be made that the treaties with foreign nations may be equally ignored. In fact, since the relationship of the states to the Congress is also included in that clause, the elimination of any one of the parties may result in a process of "legislative erosion" by which the position of the states themselves might be in jeopardy.

This insistence on the recognition of their nationhood has been viewed as evidence of either Indians' "contrariness" or, at worst, their desire to be entirely separated from the United States as a whole. It is neither.

If some common belief of all the tribes were to be sought, it would possibly be that all shared a conviction that at creation they were ordained to a special task. The Great Spirit placed them here, told them what to do and how to do it. They were to live in harmony with the earth and with the laws he gave them, taking only such of his bountiful gifts as were necessary to sustain them and thus preserve on the earth the material and spiritual perfection in which it was created.

Such a conviction is, of course, difficult to translate into the legal language of legislation; and it is sometimes infuriating to resource developers. Indians can do little at this time to "preserve" the perfection of the country as a whole; they still have the obligation to fulfill this stewardship over their own small corner of it.

The preservation of Indians' "national identity" is the framework in which they can move on to complete this obligation. Without it as an individual, the Indian is overwhelmed by a society with a totally different concept. A lonely sentinel, the Indian is bowed in sorrow before the Creator.

CHAPTER 6

The Image

Identity is one thing; Image is something else. It might be said that Image is how we are likely to be viewed by other people, and that Identity is our consciousness of self. Either of these aspects may be more important to one person than it is to another, but in some degree both concerns seem to be intrinsic to the very nature of humankind.

In the ancient teachings—and this idea was shared by other cultures of the past—it was recognized that the most healthful situation resulted when all things were in balance. As in nature, there must be sunshine and rain, growth and decay, rest and renewal. We certainly know that where an imbalance of nature exists all sorts of unpleasant things result: floods, famine, plagues of insects, the increase or extinction of one or another species to the point of endangerment of their habitat. Thus there ought to be a balance between the importance of Image and Identity. If we are concerned only with how we appear to other people, we may find ourselves in deep trouble, for the crowd does not always lead us into paths of righteousness. Or we may find it safer to do nothing at all, in fear of what "they" will say. We are out of balance in any case.

If we are so enchanted with our own identity that we have no concern for the thoughts or feelings of other people, we are way out of balance and will probably win few friends and influence fewer people.

As Indians began to emerge into visibility, they found that very often they did not match up with the general picture of what an Indian ought to be. If some were uninterested in hunting and didn't particularly care for the taste of wild meat anyhow, what kind of Indians were they? If they put aside buckskins for three-piece suits, they were hardly representative of their culture. There were various "old lettered sayings" which helped to create a stereotyped image.

"Indians don't need as much money as other people— they don't have as many expenses."

"Indians go wild when they drink. I know this is true; I had this friend in the second World War...."

"Indians have no sense of time, so they are poor workers."

"Indians have high cheek bones and very bad tempers."

Now few of us, as Indians, ever wanted to be anything other than what the Creator designed us to be; and most of us wanted to be "good" Indians. There was another old saying that we thought was going a bit too far in that aim, "The only good Indian is a dead one." We couldn't alter the cheek bones, either; but we could, by gravy, give a good performance in the other qualifications. If to be Indian was to be poorer than other people, lazier, and drunker on Friday, we'd be it with all our might and main. I don't think any of us remember exactly when we realized that the Image was getting in the way of our sense of Identity, but as more of us were moving into the job world, saw the necessity of modern health care in a world of increased population, learned to enjoy the advantages of fresh foods in winter, we began to hear comments like: "Hey! I'm not an Indian because I live in a tepee and hunt the buffalo; and I'm no less Indian if I live in a penthouse and wear a three-piece suit. I'm Indian because that's the way the Good Spirit made me."

Of course, there were some who were so enchanted with this new image that they became rather adamant about it and, having found their voices, created a few false images of their own. Some Indians use the terms "white man" and "white man's way" as derogatory epithets; and people are naturally repelled by a criticism they feel is unjustified. I have a feeling that often Indians who use these bitter commentaries do not always know what they mean by them, except as they pertain to a certain arrogance and self-interest which have all too often been Indians' experience when confronted by the dominant society. The words do not apply to their individual friends or to wives or husbands (except at times of disagreements).

Today, with our consciousness of equal opportunity and the Women's Movement, there is some resentment over the term "white man." This may be a good place to explain this discriminatory title.

In the days when the term came into general usage and became in fact such a part of our vocabulary, Indians had very little contact with white women. They were entirely aware that white women existed for captives were taken in the wars. A few of these adapted very quickly to the ways of their captors and became very good Indians, indeed. As a general rule, however, they were a lot of trouble and as often as not were transferred by circuitous routes to some neutral point where they were either sold as slaves or redeemed as hostages.

Aside from these brief encounters, white *women* did not cause the difficulties the Indian was experiencing. There were no women fighting the wars for territory. The missionaries, traders, and explorers were male. The experiences with government negotiators, agents, and pony soldiers were with white *men*. There were no white women setting policies of genocide and confiscation that so implanted the impression of a total lack of compassion that the term "white man" became synonymous with difference or "otherness."

It would seem to me that our white sisters, no matter how deeply committed they are to equal rights, might take some comfort from the fact that this is one area where equal responsibility does not apply. Now that we have so many capable women in government service, health care, and other professions, it is to be expected that our children will adopt the term "white people" — for good or ill. Historically speaking, however, the title is accurate.

During the first years of the settlement of the country, our judgments were inclined to be less hidebound. To some of the eastern tribes, white neighbors were called either "Quakels" or "Yenghees." The former term was obviously a corruption of Quaker whose reputation for honesty, square dealing, and peace was a legacy from William Penn. Yenghees were "long-knives" who were out to get the best of Indians either by political manipulation or by violence. In some such manner, we speak of the "white man's way" and feel some revulsion, except...there are some undoubted improvements we wouldn't mind having more of!

I remember Aunty Kay, a real Iroquois-matriarch type who was prone to speak succinctly and to the point. An insurance salesman once said to her, "Come, now, think of the advantages you have in civilization. Don't you think you're better off?"

"Well," she replied, "my kids can go to school; but then, they have to go—to learn how to deal with the world that you have made. But mainly what they are learning is how to outsmart their companions, how to figure faster, get more attention, more material possessions than their neighbors. In our old ways, we tried not to outdo our neighbors but to excell ourselves. There is an old prayer that says, 'I seek strength, not to be better than my brother but to fight my greatest enemy, myself.'

"Then we never had a welfare program—or needed one. It was a matter of pride to take care of our own family; but if our neighbor's crop failed, and we had more potatoes than he had, he would simply find a bag of them outside his door. We would both have been embarrassed if he had had to ask. No one ever heard of a lock on a tepee or a longhouse. Now I can't put enough locks on my door."

I hear these criticisms, and then I return to my quiet corner. My neighbor is there, my oldest friend, who has never turned her back on another's need, who would rather paint an old cupboard than to buy the finest reproduction, and who has such a store of common sense in time of trouble that she is the court of last resort in our little community.

It is when "Image" comes into conflict with "Identity" that the results are most ludicrous and at the same time often provide an avenue to a sense of balance.

I have this one son, David, who—as I have said before—has been the "strong right arm" in this family. He was eleven when Grey Owl died; three days after the funeral he cleared the old desk and carefully arranged the tools and bottles of dye as he had seen his father do. He retrieved some scraps of leather, picked up the swivel knife and proceeded to become a master craftsman. Through his first three years in high school he throttled his love of sports to dash home and produce the wallets and handbags that were our mainstay. His fine work was a challenge to his younger brothers and sisters, and by the time he reached his senior year there were other hands to fill in for him so he could have that one year to be young with his classmates. He has been, in fact, a sort of father figure for my other children who still report to him their victories and vicissitudes. For all these things, I am eternally grateful; but his most indispensable role has been that when my head is in the clouds, he can keep my feet firmly on the ground. When I become too puffed with self-importance he can, with his dry wit, bring me safely to earth.

The major part of my public speaking has involved schools, community groups, or historical societies. I began wearing buckskins because I felt more at ease, more comfortable with my subject; but I quickly learned that the regalia served two other purposes. First, there is a terrific impact on an audience when I come swinging up to the podium with all my fringes flying and, instead of saying, 'Ugh! Me heap big Injun," I am able to express myself in good, plain English. Second, there is nothing like "viva la difference!" to impress the media and thus provide you with more ears to hear the message and to assist in the accomplishment of your sponsor's purpose. I do protest that neither of these cynical by-products was my own idea; they are simply facts of life.

At any rate, I found myself receiving "journalistic scholarly degrees" as reporters tried to outdo each other in the coverage of their subject. I became consecutively (and undeservedly) "a spokesperson for the Indian cause," "a historian," "a noted historian," "a noted writer and historian," "a prime authority on Indian history and affairs." In actuality I was no smarter than I had been before. To all of these credits, David would chuckle, "Another promotion! Where will it all end?"

The climax came with a trip to Jack's Creek, Tennessee—an experience that was most precious to me because of the vitality of the congregation I was visiting, the commitment of the women of the church, and the love we all shared in those two weeks.

We had had a little discussion about my arrival. It seemed that the editor of the local paper had expressed an interest in being on the scene, and since my plane would arrive with only an hour before the news deadline, asked if I would wear the buckskins. I would! No one on the plane was impressed, but I stepped into the lounge to a barrage of flashbulbs. There were several newspaper reporters and two television crews. People getting off the plane and people waiting to embark were buzzing, "Who was on the plane?" A small boy with a toy drum and an armful of flowers came shyly to greet me while the photographers were yelling, "This way! Look this way!"

It had never happened before, and I really was not sure how well I had acquitted myself, but one reporter had had some trouble with traffic and asked for a later interview. That ought to give me time to organize my thoughts and correct any misunderstanding. Correct! The following day, headlines in her paper proclaimed *Visiting Royalty,* and she went on to describe me as "sitting cross-legged on the couch"—a feat which I am physically incapable of performing! It was so deliciously hilarious that I promptly telephoned David.

"I've just had a new promotion," I giggled.

"Oh, mom," he said wearily, "Don't tell me you're God."

At this point I began to realize that the Image was actually getting in the way of my identity. What were the buckskins saying to other people? That I was trying to be a "personality" for the cameras? That I was a "real" Indian straight from the tepee? Was I wearing them because I felt more assured within myself, or because they were in keeping with the Image?

I love buckskins. (They *are* truly comfortable—unless the wearer is scrubbing a floor or running a lathe.) They are precious to me, however, not because they represent my culture but because I had to wait so many years to get the leather and to spend so many hours that I could ill afford to do the beadwork. The whole experience made it possible for me to take a good, long look at this question of Image. Where should it begin—and end? And how does it also apply to my view of other people than my own?

First, I was brought to realize that the good women of Tennessee certainly were innocent of any misunderstanding of my purpose in being there. What we had arranged together was simply a convenience to media representatives who were going to bring to the attention of the local viewers the activity we all hoped would be a special event. The only discomfort stemmed from the bizarre overreaction that had me, of all things, "sitting cross-legged on the couch!" That left me with the ridiculous assumption that if I were not in that position I should have been—to carry out the Image.

I looked back across the years and remembered the times when the special garments were entirely appropriate—the first time I stood before a congregation to share the drama of the awakening of the Remnant. Then they were a commemoration of all those ancestors who had kept the faith that their Creator would, indeed, remember and keep them. The times when little children touched the leather with gentle hands, learning, as children do, that the world is full of adventure and of new things they have never seen before. The times I joined my people in the dance while the drums drew us into a oneness of tradition. Thus the wearing of the total regalia was best conserved for private, very special occasions. I have dwelt on this at some length, because I suspect other Indians have had similar experiences and it has influenced a new dress code. We dress, as any sensible person would, for the occasion, with the proviso that we are allowed some latitude for our own personal style and taste. One highly successful Indian woman in Washington wears conventional clothes that are appropriate to her office. She also wears her hair in braids and the beadwork for which her tribe is noted. She says, "These visible signs of your heritage should not be something you just put on for show, but because they are right for you. You should be consistent."

A retired army colonel, throughout his long career, wore a string of turquoise, carefully concealed beneath his undergarment when he was in uniform. He said, "I feel naked without it."

I have heard younger women say that they "absolutely swoon" at the sight of well-wrapped braids above a three-piece business suit. Having passed the age of swooning, I can neither confirm nor deny this effect; one must admit, however, the style has flair. My own opinion is that this modified dress code is the most refreshing thing that has come along in years. It allows us to express our own sense of identity and our ability to project that identity into the twentieth century. By the same token, we can weave a rug, make a bowl, hunt, fish, and do beadwork not just to "preserve our culture" but because either that's what we do best or it is what is available in our habitat. Any housewife who has stood over a hot stove would recognize that baking in an outside oven in a hot climate is the sensible thing to do.

So...what of the image Indian people have had of the "white man" or the "white man's path"? I have looked in vain for the mysterious "they" who fit the description. There are, indeed, corporations and cartels that simply are blind to any right except their own right to profit. There are, indeed, people who are arrogant and lifted in pride. There *are* those who, like the early "Yenghees," *will* have their way by any means.

And then there are the Quakels—honest, decent, kind folk who go above and beyond the call of duty to lighten a burden, dry a tear, lift a spirit, or plant a rose in the pit of despair.

In California I visited the headquarters of the Wycliffe Bible Institute. There committed men and women study the mechanics of language so they can go into the darkest, most isolated areas of the world and master languages that have never been learned before. They work out a system of phonetic writing for people who have no written language, translate the scriptures, and teach the people to read for themselves the word of God. What an inspiring act of devotion!

There is the Genesis Project, a monumental undertaking originally instituted by a group of Hebrew scholars but now involving many Christian churches as they move into the New Testament. Those who are a part of it regard themselves as "a company of people committed to putting the Bible back into twentieth century life, using the contemporary media of motion pictures." There are hundreds and hundreds of thousands of young people in this country alone who have never opened a Bible—nor, indeed, has anyone ever pointed out to them their need to do so. They are, however, subjected daily to the violence of TV and fourth-rate motion pictures. Without some exposure to the knowledge that the love of God is there for all people, how will they seek it? How shall they choose a righteous, happier path if they do not know it exists? If the Genesis Project succeeds in its aims, it may touch the lives of these who have never been reached and call them to receive a fuller ministry.

These spectacular undertakings are but the tip of the iceberg. If the uncounted volunteer workers in every field of social service and all the people committed to the eradication of world hunger and world violence are considered it would seem that there are more Quakels than Yenghees. Yet one atheist was strong enough to force through legislation which denies children the right to a few quiet moments of prayer as they begin their school day—a privilege, for some strange reason, granted to congressmen.

I am impressed by these long-unsung aspects of the white man's path. Perhaps, if we all care enough, have enough love and commitment, we shall be able to get rid of these false images and assume our true and mutual identity as children of one Father.

I am convinced that both aspects, Image and Identity, have deep significance in a healthy society. The prisons and the drug rehabilitation centers are full of people who got the wrong start because they did not care what other people thought. The individual is ill indeed who has no sense of self-worth. In Indian life, any grandfather will remember that his growing-up years were filled with admonishments: "Do not do that; people will think you were badly raised. It reflects ill upon your people." "Do not act so; it is beneath you."

The surest bulwark against temptation, of course, is so to live that we reflect credit on the God who made us in his image; but self-respect will go a long way in that direction, too.

CHAPTER 7

This Old House

If you should happen to be traveling east or west, and if you can bring yourself to get off the super-highway, you may stumble across Ohio 40, which is the original pioneer route to the west. Somewhere along the line you are bound to arrive in Brownsville, which has no particular designation as to being either town or village but which has a long and interesting history.

Many of its citizens' ancestors settled the Refugee Tracts allocated to those who had lost property or provided some service in the Revolutionary War. They have tales to tell of days when periodically the Indians descended to drive the horses off, whooping with glee at this harassment of the settlement. These pranks seem not to have occasioned any lasting bitterness on either side. The settlers simply rounded up a stray mount or two, brought back the herd, and everybody settled down until the next time.

Brownsville was, in fact, a thriving little community, one of the original coach stops through the wilderness. The coach stop building is as sturdy as ever it was, though it has not for many years been operated as an inn. Now the town has settled into comfortable retirement. The little eccentricities of its people provide a gentle spice, but the days march serenely by, enlivened only by the occasional ambulance sent to pick up an elderly patient, and by the half dozen or so young rapscallions who gather nightly on the bench in front of the one store.

Halfway along the single street that comprises most of the town is a nondescript little house of no particular style or vintage that is, to me, the most precious spot in all this precious land. It was home to my young Indians growing up; it is my haven and refuge in these, my winter years.

Your first impression of the cottage might well be that it is in the process of being swallowed by a giant maple. One of the last survivors of the noble trees that once lined the street, it has branches that spread across the roof to tap gently during storms.

The underpinnings of the porch have settled wearily, having known the racing feet of many children going in and out. The old boards have collapsed into senility so that one of the roof supports has given up the battle and now rests from its labors at the side of the house. There is nothing dreary about this prospect, however, for above the entrance hangs a weathered sign: "Those who enter here are strangers but once."

I always have to enter by the back door when I return from my travels. As a concession to modern ways, I lock the front door; the kitchen door is never locked, for it is known to all that this is a house of love where they may rest and be refreshed. Curiously, since this has become general knowledge, I have never found one item disturbed, though the current fad of vandalism has touched other places in the area.

I strongly suspect that would-be looters take one look and assume, rightly, that there is nothing worth bothering with, though perhaps that is unkind. It is much more likely that the house is its own protection, for it exudes such an aura of love and welcome that the most coldhearted vandal would certainly be embarrassed to disturb its sleepy peace.

This old house and I have been through many vicissitudes together, and we understand one another very well. It has a monumental patience. Once upon a spring shower, there began a steady song of running water.

"Something is very wrong," said I to myself. "How could water be running in a house that has no water?"

The hunt for the source of this phenomenon took me into a part of the house that I had never seen, the crawl space under the eaves. Sure enough, there was a hole as big as a fist through which I could see passing clouds.

"Oh, well, if that's all," I said. "Hold still and Manna fix."

My grandson's plastic bathtub which he had long outgrown, fit perfectly under the hole, and has done good service these many moons. Occasionally, in moments of irascibility, when there is a spell of windy, rainy weather, the house mutters: *"When* are you going to get this roof fixed?"

"Hush!" I return. "It's not every house that has a built-in humidity system."

Sometimes, when I have had weeks of high and heady experiences, when so many people have flattered and spoiled me and I am very full of myself, I am consumed with a hunger for this place. The longest miles are those that bring me home.

I have at last convinced the family that for those first hours of homecoming, I want to be alone. My bags are deposited in the living room, groceries taken to the kitchen, and we are blissfully alone in our private world, my house and I. Those first hours I want to do nothing but to wander about, soaking up the quiet peace. I climb the little old-fashioned winding stairs to the boys' rooms, the area we called "the Reservation." A pair of ice skates still hangs on the wall, a football still rests on the bookshelves. The dresser drawers are full of sweat shirts and jeans which they will probably never want, but which just might come in handy if the crew comes home.

Everywhere I turn, everything I do wakes precious memories. The windows need to be washed, which brings up the inconvenience of carrying water—and the memory of the sweetest time of our lives.

To attempt to rear seven children without a father and on an infinitesimal income, I found, was to be always ten steps behind. There was never enough time, never enough money. Shoes fell apart at inconvenient moments, and I was torn with the need to anticipate and prepare for questions that really needed a father's answers. Various and sundry problems developed; repairs that once would have been magically taken care of became unconquerable foes.

When, in the midst of this, I suddenly stumbled onto people who had so much love to give that they were able to look beyond the shabby physical aspect of my life and reach out with tenderness to help lift the burden, the shock was almost more than I could bear.

We should have long since joined some identifiable group—a church, a community club. We had many excuses. We never all had decent shoes at the same time. There was usually someone in sick bay. We had no transportation. I saw people going about their churchly duties, dedicated and devoted, but closed in their private little world in which there seemed no place for us. We were all avid students of the scriptures, and our frequent conversations were opening young minds to many searching questions about our Father's purpose for his world.

There was, however, a fetter that bound us to the experiences of our people; and Indian experiences with Christianity had not been entirely happy ones. Rightly or wrongly, the overall impression we had gained was that we just couldn't be Christian without rejecting our Indian heritage. Indians were dark—and therefore accursed. They had strange rituals and were said to worship the sun or other manifestations of nature. Lacking neighborhood schools, Indian children had been sent into mission schools, often to emerge equipped neither to face the outside world nor to return to their own. We were constantly besieged by no doubt well-meaning Christians who thought we should be happy to have them take our children to rear.

There were all these ideas and more, so when we felt the hunger to worship with others there was an equal reluctance to give way to the one thing that might sever our final ties with our people. Then—like a sudden shaft of sun through storm clouds—this door to light was swung open for us. It did entirely change the course of our lives, but it brought us closer to the precious things of our own culture than we could have dreamed.

We found a church whose people had so much love to give that it literally engulfed us and swept away all doubts. It was a love that accepted us as we were—broken shoes, beads, and feathers...or whatever. It was a love that was able to laugh heartily at problems and have at them, a love that would not be put off by our doubts.

Then, in this house, began a demonstration of what these people truly believed—that love was giving of themselves, of their time, their talents, and their substance. The cars rolled in one day, and out poured a bevy of the elders of the church—men I formerly had seen in shirts and ties, freshly scrubbed, and very dignified. Now, in overalls and sturdy work shoes, they plowed into the mud surrounding the nonfunctioning well pump. Happily, they dragged up incredible lengths of pipe; gleefully they bent their heads over the motor.

The women came with curtains and affectionate chatter, and we cooked a feast. It was like home—everyone working together with much laughter and good will. Someone knew how to pipe water into the kitchen; someone knew how to make the electric connections. One couple, who had reared their family and now were in more comfortable circumstances, brought new linoleum and also built a huge and sturdy cupboard.

And when all was finished they gave more precious gifts—the opening of the door to truth, an understanding of the special place for our people in the Master's plan, a wider vision of an expanding universe of the Creator's love.

Later, of course, the well went dry, and we again had to carry water; but that took not one iota from the precious memory. Some of that atmosphere of love, of caring enough, I believe, sank into the walls of this old house so that it dreams through its declining years of all that passed within them. It folded me close during the years I took the witness I had received and built it into a wall of evidence that would perhaps one day help to bring our people back to the wisdom of their fathers. It brings me back to earth with a sense of humility, knowing that every witness is important, but only as a part of the whole tide that will one day love all of us back into the kingdom of God.

So the time comes when I pack the bags for another

journey. The house lifts one eyelid in resignation. "Off again, I see. Well, greet the children if you see them, and tell them I wish to goodness they'd come home."

"God bless you, house," I say. "Maybe this summer I'll fix that roof."

House chuckles and goes to sleep.

CHAPTER 8

The New Heroes

Or "Cheer up! Things are always darkest before they turn totally black." — Dan's law

There is one event in Indian history about which I receive more questions than any other—possibly because it is mentioned in more history books, possibly because it has received more recent publicity.

I include it here because it has generated more evidence of the bizarre processes of the modern "think tank" than any that I have encountered in "lo these many moons." The final episode of this tragic event has been carefully swept under the rug. The implications may affect our children long after the reasoning behind them has been lost to memory.

We have made a great fuss these last years about getting at the truth of history. Everyone is willing to admit that written history is most often just one opinion and that truth is only fact viewed from one side of the fence. Armies of debunkers stand ready to slash and prune, stripping the "fancy foliage" from popular heroes. In fact, this unmasking of heroes has become such popular sport that it begins to seem our erstwhile idols not only had feet of clay but were clay from head to foot.

In common with most Americans of my generation I considered George Washington a hero to emulate—the very soul of honor, entirely noble in manner and mores in the best sense of the words. I was a bit hazy on just what he had done to merit the title "Father of his country," but the fact that he was willing to take a licking rather than to lie about the vandalism of his father's cherry tree—well! That was something to set the dreams stirring. If a boy loved truth to the extent that he was willing to suffer for it, he might grow up to be president, live in a beautiful mansion on the river, and go down in history as a great American.

It was something to bring the head up, the shoulders back. The fact that it was a cherry tree was merely incidental but added an extra dimension to the tale. We knew about cherry trees. Cherry trees were dawn-pink clouds in spring where robins nested. Cherry trees produced the luscious pies mama baked, their tops lacy with pastry like fancy valentines. It was a terrible thing for young George to do and, I strongly suspect, acted as a serious deterrent to similar crimes on our part.

Now we are told that not only did George Washington not thus distinguish himself as an advocate of truth as a boy, but the whole story was a tissue of lies. Now that the experts have "freed" us from this fable, we can of course go on to viewing a Washington thigh deep in a veritable national debt of wines and rich viands while his men bled shoeless in the snow at Valley Forge.

The real truth, as usual, probably lies somewhere between. There is no doubt in my mind that George Washington, whatever else he was or was not, was a man of his word. Whether the incident of the cherry tree ever happened, very probably as a lad he was taught to tell the truth. Whole generations of grandfathers can testify that punishment for telling a lie was swift and sure—and drastic. There was simply no offense of childhood more likely to result in a summons to the woodshed than was lying. Of course, that was before the days of child psychology and free expression. The woodshed was standard equipment for growing boys; it housed frequent effective, if rough, counseling sessions.

To pursue the Washington family a bit further, I have discovered obscure historical accounts of a heretofore shadowy Martha who loaded her carriage with such delicacies as Mount Vernon produced, as well as such necessities as she could lay hands on, popping up at her husband's headquarters to dispense cheer and largesse. I always wondered about Martha, an imaginative woman who ordered a king-sized bed for her tall husband. The unmaskers haven't reached her yet...but they will!

The debunking goes on. It is now unfashionable to mention the days when Blacks were "Negras" and enslaved. We may even forget that this cancer ever existed. We may cease to think it in any way extraordinary that a Booker T. Washington or a George Carver or any of the other Black heroes emerged from the hopeless condition of slavery to inspire other peoples in times of deep despair.

In the mid-70s the idiocy of this great debunking campaign was directed at the Wounded Knee Massacre. During the confrontation between members of the American Indian Movement and federal troops at Wounded Knee, South Dakota, in 1973 there was much discussion in Congress on the stance of the opposing sides. On March 14, 1973, the Speaker of the House recognized "the gentleman from New York, Mr. Robison" who was granted five minutes to present his views for the *Congressional Record.* After briefly reviewing the currrent situation, he asked that the description of the original event in 1890, as narrated by the National Park Service in its publication "Soldier and Brave," be inserted in the daily record.

The article contains a review of the events leading up to the final confrontation which is described as "more a massacre than a battle; serving as an example of national guilt for the mistreatment of Indians."

The Ghost Dance Religion had captured the imagination of Indian people in its hope of renewed power and invincible protection. Soon....soon it would happen that the white-eyes would disappear from the land. Soon would come the Rejuvenator to restore the earth to harmony once more and the people to their ancient ways.

It was an exasperating turn of events from the point of view of those in the military, and their consensus was that it must be broken up at all costs, its leaders dispersed and confined. Accordingly, a detachment of troops was ordered to the Pine Ridge Reservation to arrest Chief Sitting Bull at his home. During the course of this risky business, he was shot and killed by the Indian Police assigned to the actual removal of this respected holy man of the Hunkpapa Sioux.

Whatever other effect the death of Sitting Bull produced, it was a foreshadowing of the factions and divisions that were to develop in later years. The question would forever lurk in the back of the minds of Indians when faced with those of their people who walked the white man's path: "Whose side are you on, anyhow?"

The immediate result was to inflame the Hunkpapa, and 200 of them fled southward to the Cheyenne River to become allied with Chief Hump and the Miniconjou. It was a coalition doomed never to get off the ground, for within a short time Hump and his 400 followers and all but thirty-eight of the Hunkpapa Sioux surrendered at Fort Bennett, South Dakota.

This small, hard core of resisters and a group led by Chief Big Foot enjoyed a last few days of defiance. Big Foot was ill with pneumonia; his people were ragged and hungry. He informed the military authorities that on a certain day he would capitulate. Meanwhile, he was desperately ill. Let there be these last days of communion together in the Ghost Dance. The people huddled in the snow-shrouded tepees. Only the hope that at the last possible moment the miracle would happen, only this hope could have sustained them.

Whether Big Foot was too ill to give the order to move, whether Yellow Bird, the Medicine Man, was able to reaffirm their faith in their invincibility, or whether they were simply operating on what today we call "Indian time," the appointed day came and went and no Indians appeared for their rendezvous.

On December 28, a Seventh Cavalry detachment under Major Samuel M. Whiteside was dispatched to intercept and deliver the band. He located his objective at Porcupine Creek, just five miles from Wounded Knee Creek, which Big Foot had designated as the place where he would surrender peacefully.

So far, so good. And now, as the saying goes, the feathers hit the fan.

Col. James W. Forsyth arrived at Wounded Knee to supervise the movement of the captives to Omaha. Backed by a force of 500 men, including the entire Seventh Cavalry Regiment, a company of Oglala

Scouts, and an artillery detachment, he was going to have no nonsense.

Here the account entered into the *Congressional Record* gives the climax. If I choose to present this account rather than the Indian version of the event, it is to demonstrate that until now, this is the account bearing the endorsement of the Federal Government taken from military records.

The disarming occured the next day. It was not a wise decision, for the Indians had shown no inclination to fight and regarded their guns as cherished possessions and means of livelihood. Between the tepees and the soldiers' tents was the council ring. On a nearby low hill a Hotchkiss battery had its guns trained directly on the Indian camp. The troops, in two cordons, surrounded the council ring.

The warriors did not comply readily with the request to yield their weapons, so a detachment of troops went through the tepees and uncovered about 40 rifles. Tension mounted, for the soldiers had upset the tepees and disturbed women and children; and the officers feared the Indians were still concealing firearms. Meanwhile, the militant medicine man Yellow Bird had circulated among the men urging resistance and reminding them that their ghost-shirts made them invulnerable. The troops attempted to search the warriors and the rifle of one, Black Coyote, considered by many members of his tribe to be crazy, apparently discharged accidentally when he resisted. Yellow Bird gave a signal for retaliation and several warriors leveled their rifles at the troops and may even have fired them. The soldiers, reacting to what they deemed to be treachery, sent a volley into the Indian ranks. In a brief but frightful struggle, the combatants ferociously wielded rifle, knife, revolver, and war club.

Soon the Hotchkiss guns opened fire from the hill, indiscriminately mowing down some of the women and children who had gathered to watch the proceedings. Within minutes, the field was littered with Indian dead and wounded; tepees were burning; and Indian survivors were scrambling in panic to the shelter of nearby ravines pursued by the soldiers and raked with fire from the Hotchkiss guns. The bodies of men, women and children were found scattered for a distance of 2 miles from the scene of the first encounter.

There is more—an accounting of dead and wounded,

the assessment of the result—but this is enough for our purposes here. Enough, especially, when on-the-scene reporting in 1890 became a part of the military record. Enough, when photographs exist of a gaunt Big Foot pointing in death a bony finger at his foes, the bodies of women and children sprawled in the snow. But now, in this enlightened age, the debunkers are at work, busily rewriting history.

In 1975 Senator James G. Abourezk (Democrat, South Dakota) long considered a proponent of Indian rights, in an effort to assuage the recurrent angry memories of this sorry chapter of history, introduced a bill that would pay cash benefits in the total amount of $600,000 to the descendants of the Sioux who died at Wounded Knee. The bill met with horrified oppostion. What? Death benefits to American Indians? What a Pandora's box of trouble that could be!

One of the arguments advanced against this settlement of death benefits to the Sioux was that it might set a precedent. Indubitably! From the massacre of Christian Delaware Indians in 1792 to the Long Walk of the Navajo and the Trail of Tears of the Cherokee, history is rife with the tragic incidents of a war for extermination.

And when we get through with the claims of Indians, how about the Blacks, who had some reason to complain also? Good grief, we'd be up to our necks in claims! We protest that, after all, these things happened long before our time, but we have an atavistic tingle of dread over the "sins of the fathers," realizing that we are now the "fourth and fifth generation."

Everything is going to be all right, however. We have some new "heroes" in the persons of a team of military experts who promptly dashed to the rescue with a study which decreed that, after all, the Indians fired first, so it was entirely to be expected that both innocent and guilty should be exterminated—and certainly not be entitled to any sympathy or redress.

The implication is that if we don't like the heat we can simply flood the kitchen. A little manipulation here and there can lead to the idea that it wasn't really hot—just pleasantly warm.

The truth is that the soldiers were under orders to perform a nasty chore; they were under the command of a hothead out to make "Brownie points," and all 500 of them were probably scared to death. It doesn't take much imagination to conclude that at the accidental firing of a weapon the whole kit and kaboodle of them panicked.

Let's get some straight thinking here. Is it all right, in a moment of fear, to slay the innocent with the guilty? For that matter, what sort of regiment was it that was unable to disarm "one Indian—thought to be crazy"? And who trained the Hotchkiss battery boys on the target range?

The real truth is that there were no heroes at Wounded Knee. There was a sick and ragged bunch of Indians, not trying to be heroes, just waiting to surrender...and an army out of control.

This army study should start a whole new trend. First off, we don't want to hear any more about Mai Lai. After all, there *were* probably Viet Cong in that village, armed to the teeth. Since it's impossible to tell the difference between friend and enemy, why not get rid of all of them? We might have saved a lot of money on the treatment offered to the scarred survivors of Nagasaki. It wasn't *our* fault they were caught in the blast. Their condemnation lay in the fact of their presence when the bomb was dropped.

Ridiculous? Of course. The manipulation of history

after the fact has excused the inexcusable and made "heroes" of some very unheroic people; it has also destroyed some heroes we'd have been well-advised to keep. The truth is that our children need heroes—men and women who set standards for courage, justice, compassion, and the moral fiber that we hope best characterize Americans. To face the truth that heroes are just men and women caught in a moment of glory should not detract from the ideals they teach. The truth is that men fight for their ideals be they right or wrong, whether they are inconvenient to the enemy or not. Nations and individuals commit sins against even their own consciences.

The beating of breasts, the wringing of hands, the wearing of sackcloth and ashes do not assuage either individual or national guilt. To face the truth, rather than to cover it, to bind the wounds, rather than to deny that they exist, to repent and sin no more—these are the sharp, two-edged swords that alone can heal the battle scars of man's past excesses.

CHAPTER 9

Home Is the Hunter

The soft old boards of the porch are warm under my moccasins; the earth steams a little beneath the sun. Slow crystal drops form on the maple tree, dripping from neat holes drilled by a small sapsucker intent on his harvest.

We have been locked for weeks in an unusually severe cycle of ice and snow. A few days ago every blade of grass, every shrub, and the tallest trees were a fairyland of silver and white. Each tiny branch was etched in white against the gray canvas of the sky.

Our yard is the only one in the neighborhood that is not clipped and mowed. I take no credit for this, not wishing to embarrass my neighbors by presenting an untidy negative in the midst of their positive neat green lawns. It is just that I and the lawn mower seem to have worn out at the same time. I must admit, however, that is simply a lame excuse and I get a secret satisfaction from wild grasses springing.

There is a feeling of insistent life in the air and underfoot. Tiny roots shake away their sleep and chorus, "Push."

It is the first time in months I have set foot in my garden, what with the ice and the long trek across the country. I can trace the once wide boundaries of it by the different growth of weeds. I think that years from now someone may say, "There's been a garden here." Now I stand remembering how the bounty of the Lord was poured out on this spot. All summer long we bore great loads of vegetables into the house. The cupboard shelves began to overflow with jars of brightly colored beans and tomatoes and carrots.

How long ago it seems when in that first wild grief I cried, "God help me! What shall I do to feed these children?" and heard the answer in a loving voice that whispered in my heart, "I'll help."

Now that the children are scattered like last autumn's leaves, the garden plot is only half its former size. Surrounding it are the little stakes where I strung a rope to hold many white streamers in a vain hope of discouraging the local rabbit from eating my beans.

He had eaten two rows and I was beginning to protest his gluttony. A neighbor advised putting red pepper on the leaves—a sure deterrent, she said. It seemed a rather drastic cure and, not having any red pepper, I sprinkled the leaves generously with chili powder. The rabbit signaled his approval of the seasoning by finishing the whole planting. After he had expressed his gratitude by eating the second planting as well, I gave up and set the whole plot with tomato plants which were not to his taste.

Poor fellow, I sadly fear he has met with disaster. There was a great outcry and thrashing of bushes along the brook some days ago. Three of the neighborhood lads carrying .22 rifles were wildly dashing here and there.

"We lost a rabbit," they chorused. "We're sure we hit it, but it's disappeared."

Doubting very much whether a well-placed shot from a .22 would have left much to get away, I retreated, hoping the little guy had found more hospitable quarters elsewhere.

Soon the shaded places under the maple will be ankle deep in tiny vines with miniature scalloped leaves and bluebell shaped flowers. David knows the name of this lush carpet; for me it is enough to lie in the sweet, damp woodsy fragrance of it.

There are not hours left in life to soak up the loveliness of this earth, nor hours left to see the thousand-thousand glories across the Beloved Land. But there is time today for that one special, precious place called — for obvious reasons — Flint Ridge, which lies across a hill to northward of our village.

The Place of the Flint is bisected by a country road running east and west, but both sides, north and south, are state park areas. Those many years ago when we first came the southern part was closed to visitors. On the north were many shaded little paths, literally paved with tiny chips of flint. Great boulders lay on either side, and dank leaf-filled hollows marked the ancient work pits.

Our children ran the paths or sat quietly at our feet while their father spun the golden tales of ancient times. Often we stood beside the road and looked with longing to the south, for he would say that there his people had encamped, and there would be the very earth on which they walked.

There is tradition that in very ancient times this place knew many battles, for the people had become greedy and full of self-interest. Here on this ridge, the flint lay exposed and was obviously the place the Great Spirit had ordained that his children could take material for their spearpoints and arrows. No Indian would have dreamed of tearing open the breast of the Earth Mother, so mining would have been unthinkable.

Thus when they began quarreling over the possession of this anciently ordained source there came, once upon a summer, the voice of the Thunderbird speaking in anger a threat from above. Quarrels must cease or, with lightning and thunder, the place of the flint would be blasted forever. So it came about that the ridge became neutral ground, where all of the nations could share in this gift of the Creator. One day's journey approaching and one day's travel in leaving, all warfare must cease.

It must have been a fantastic scene. Tribes from north and south, from east and west, copper ornaments and eagle feathers, river pearls and seashells, bright plumes from the southland—what a picture they must have presented!

Did the women trade patterns and chatter softly as they worked? Did the men tell tales of giant bears and fierce panthers? Did the children run laughing from camp to camp to be fed at strangers' fires?

Once my David, roaming the countryside, climbed the highest hill. A mile or so from the ridge it rises cone-like to an awesome height. There he found the stones that spoke of ancient councils. What a day that was for him—to stand suspended there between the earth and sky and know that once his father's fathers sat in council on these stones!

Some years ago, by state decree, the south side was opened to the public. The north was destitute of flint; there was not much to see, for visitors had carried off the tiny chips, and in the night someone would come with dynamite to blast the larger outcroppings.

Now a small but very good museum had been built to

the south. There was to be an opening day with speeches and a formal ribbon cutting. We were all wild with excitement. At last, at last, we would see those secret places hidden in the forest. In honor of the event—and just in case the spirits of the ancestors might peep through the veil that separated us from them—we wore our beads and fringes.

Curious glances followed us as we joined the crowd filing into the once forbidden area. Soon we realized, from the uneasy expressions on the faces of the committee, that we were a painful embarrassment to them. Many very important people had come that day to present their speeches of welcome; and here were Indians, dressed to the nines, standing in the audience! What would they do with us in an already over-crowded program? It was a bit difficult to ignore the presence of seven young Indians and their mother, gaily bedecked.

We solved their problem neatly by slipping quietly away, and thereby had the best of the bargain. While the crowd stood in the heat reflected from the concrete walkway, we were deep in the forest, reveling in the sight of great pits that once were lodge sites. We could picture them as they would have been. The pit would have been dug, the floor smoothed. Pliant, slender poles would have been sunk into the inner sides and lashed together at the tops. Branches and leaves or hides for a cover and an earthwork embankment to carry off the rain—how plain it was!

Giant trees laced overhead. Not a piece of flint was disturbed. Dan, who had performed the impossible by learning the art of arrow point-making without a teacher, reached to pick up one piece of flint. I could not find it in my heart to stop him, but I was very proud when later he approached the curator of the museum.

Bravely he met the man's eye, that keeper of the flint.

He held the fragment on his open palm and asked, "May I have this?"

For one moment only the man hesitated. Then he patted the boy's shoulder. "You surely may, son," he said. "You surely may." I think his eyes were bright with unshed tears.

Oh, for the years to tell the white glory of sun and wind and secret places where the lady-slipper blows! Oh, for the words to tell of the great migrations, the pride, and the strength of the people! And oh, for the years to search out the truth of the legends. Now in this fullness of time, they stir like the grasses in springtime, the roots chiming a chorus, "Push! Push into life again."

Now I sit on a boulder of flint grown smooth by the wind and the rain. In memory I see the bright faces of my children surrounding me. I take once again a crushed handful of flowers, and I rest in the healing, life-giving medicine of dappled sun and fragrant earth.

CHAPTER 10

Of Indian Blood

The information came in a routine report from the Coalition of Eastern Native Americans (CENA) just before I left Ohio for a series of television appearances.

"The Shawnee Nation United Remnant Band is alive and well," I told the viewers in the Indianapolis area, "and their headquarters is here in your city." It was a joyful piece of news, for I had long suspected that there were a good many Indians unaccounted for. I had received letters from some of them for whom I had no answers, no factual information.

"So far as I know, our family has always lived in Pennsylvania" (or Virginia, or Kentucky). "I know that my grandparents were Indian. I long to know their people—my people. Am I Indian—or what?"

In the tragic years of the dispersal of our people, nation after nation was torn asunder, separated and fragmented. When we speak of the "removal" of the Delaware, Cherokee, Shawnee, and other nations, we are inclined to think of great concourses of people making an uninterrupted journey—one straight shot into the sunset.

Actually, it didn't happen that way. The Delaware, driven from the missionary towns among the rolling hills of east Ohio, traveled northward to the Hurons. There, after further difficulties, some went north across the border, some west, moving and stopping here and there, to Kansas, then to Texas, and at last to Oklahoma; and with each move they lost part of their people along the way. Some of the ill were left behind; some crept into the friendly wilderness; many died. Others, however, survived though separated from their nations. A few were taken in by sympathetic white families and in time married into those communities.

There were those who managed to survive in villages and others who drifted to the developing towns and cities. Many of their children show the heritage of paler skin from white parentage; but often in their homes the tales were told of days gone by when all their nation was united.

The unique position of the tribes under the United States Constitution is that their relationship with the federal government is as tribal entities; programs for education and development are based on the eligibility of the tribes. The Reorganization Act of 1934 set certain standards by which the federal government recognized the legal status of a tribe. In time, we came to think that all Indians existed in the files of the Bureau of Indian Affairs and were to be found only in the corners designated "Reservation land." Now and then the census showed an increase in our numbers, but officially these remnants were ignored.

Among the children of these lost was kept alive the sweet traditions of their fathers. A burning pride was often nursed in secret and a hunger for others of their kind. Now, in the fullness of time, the scattered remnants were awakening. They were beginning to stand in pride and say, "Brothers, we are here!" Forgotten or ignored by state and federal governing bodies alike, theirs had been a history of total neglect.

Until a very few years ago there was no hope for these "displaced" Indians. The passage of Public Law 83-280 was an attempt to transfer to the states some of the responsibility for services, but neither they nor the Indian communities were entirely happy with the arrangement. In any case, there was no provision for those not enrolled in an eligible tribe. Neither black nor white nor recognized Indian, they constituted too small a minority even to qualify for equal opportunity. They were the "leftovers" when all the equal rights were established.

Then suddenly the dreams awoke and the lost said to each other: "We are of the people; if no one else recognizes this fact, we ourselves know it. If we never have anything else, we will hold fast to this knowledge: we are *Indian.*"

So there began, here and there, to be a strange, new seeking...a search of memories of tales told by a mother or a grandfather. Yellowed papers tucked in a Bible, old records, tribal rolls, began to define old relationships. They were able to define not only their tribal heritage but their clans, rituals, language. Their very poverty and ostracism had preserved a surprising amount of the ancient culture. They began to reach out to one another, and they learned that although they would still be unrecognized by the government they could incorporate as organizations and regain the legal right to their ancient tribal names.

There were others, sadly enough, who knew so little of their original culture that they were forced to resort to the conjectures of quasi historians, and who came up with rituals so bizarre as to arouse the dismay of more established Indian communities. Nevertheless, it was a means of enlivening the spirits of these forgotten pockets of misery, and instituted some brave plans for education, culture centers, and employment.

The Pamunkey in Virginia, once thought to be extinct, had to be a strong people or they would not have survived two centuries of heartbreaking struggle. Chippewa, Cherokee, displaced Seneca were finding new life under the help and encouragement of the Coalition of Eastern Native Americans. The aims and purposes of this fine organization were to assist the emerging tribes to assess their needs and resources and to decide for themselves which programs they desired for their people. Once the decision was made to the satisfaction of the band, their own people were given training in the administration of the projects, and assistance was provided to obtain grants and expertise to bring the dream to fulfillment.

Among these emerging bands, the problems that beset the rest of the Indian population were often magnified. Having for so long been separated, some of them were so aggressively Indian as to constitute an embarrassment to the rest of the race. More established tribes were concerned with water and land rights, schools, health services, and housing development programs, all of which brought them into relationship with the white community. Most of the leaders of established tribes were trained businessmen or educated in some professional field. They were inclined to look with slight patience at the flaunting of Indian names or the wearing of "pow-wow garments" during daily activities. Comfortably settled into their national identity, they could ignore the fact that these manifestations were a waving of banners, a proud proclamation.

These "new Indians" had, after all, something very

important to offer to their race. They may not have known the answers—who did?—but, by George, they knew the issues. They had lived with them—they and their fathers—and it took rare courage to stand up and be counted, to choose to be Indian with all the frustrations and disadvantages.

They had another value; they were an excellent test of whether it was possible to maintain a culture pattern and a good relationship with the outer community as well.

During my years in Ohio, I heard again and again the wistful question from my white neighbors: "Where are Ohio's Indians?" The last eastern headquarters of the Shawnee and the home of the great Tecumseh were in central Ohio. It was heartwarming to find that the Shawnee Nation United Remnant Band was to be reestablished in the old homeplace at Yellow Springs. With the acquisition of the first few acres, they went before the citizens of the town to ask for the understanding of their white neighbors. They had much to offer in assisting with youth activities and in sharing the values by which they intended to live.

Citizens of the nearby town of Xenia, Ohio, so nearly destroyed by a tornado, determined that in rebuilding they would have a city that reached out to help others—one that would fully recognize the worth of persons. Their cash gift was the sole means of getting the tribal office in operation during the difficult phase of transition. It was heartbreaking that before these purposes could be carried out the band was to split apart through power-struggles and through mistaken rituals that would have had Tecumseh booting them out of camp. It was increasingly plain that rebuilding a culture was going to be very difficult without access to its roots.

There was another category coming into its own. These were the isolated pockets of predominately full-blooded Indians who, for one reason or another, were either not informed about or failed to act on the Reorganization Act. Under new rulings they then began reorganizing under a charter, holding elections and otherwise conforming to the criteria set forth in the Act. A few of these have been placed on federal status and thus became eligible for federal programs and funding. It has been an uphill fight all the way, but the tribal offices hum with vitality.

Few of these programs have been available to the remnant bands, of course. They have been able to secure private grants, manpower assistance, but for the most part they are very much on their own for the acquisition of a land base or the personnel to carry out their projects.

There remains one group to be accounted for—the Urban Indians. Many of them, of course, are bona fide members of their respective tribes—people who, for one reason or another, pursue their careers in the "outer world." Among them, however, are many very good Indians whose parents or grandparents paid a terrible price for yielding to the blandishments of sociologists.

During the 1950s the Relocation Program brought numerous Indians into the cities. It seemed a good thing because there was hunger on the reservation. The population was growing and there were no jobs. The kind goverment would pay their way to the city, help them find a job and a place to live. Maybe they could make a lot of money and help the old folks at home. It was sad that so few read the fine print. There was a limit to the government's responsibility. What happened when they were entirely on their own in a world that had small patience with the untrained, where competition for jobs was an item to be reckoned with, and where the mounting cost of living swallowed up the income from the limited types of work available to them?

If we knew the whole truth, we would probably see such a demonstration of "Indian culture" as would touch the heart. When a hunter goes out for meat, he hates to return empty-handed. No one likes to admit defeat. Many of those who stayed, sank into the invisibility of poverty. They survived but just barely. As the children came along, of *course* their parents intended to enroll them; but maybe next year they could get a car and go home in style. Maybe next year they would have the time, the gas, everyone would have good shoes, and they could take along something for a feast. And sometimes it never happened, and the children were never registered.

One of the controversies that has occupied the attention of both government agencies and the Indian communities for many years has been "degree of blood." As programs for education and job opportunities arose, the question of eligibility naturally followed. Water rights and the development of resources were not—and are not—just fun and games or even just a means of "civilizing the Indian." They are vital necessities to preserve not only the culture but the very lives of the people. Indian preference for jobs in Indian Affairs is not a means of denying a non-Indian a job. It is a means of seeing that young Indians have the training, experience, and understanding to deal with the unique problems that face their own people. Who and what will qualify for the funding which is already stretched to breaking point?

This situation, already in existence, would be complicated by the emergence of large numbers of people claiming to be Indian but having no positive identification. It was becoming increasingly necessary to have a firm ruling on the whole question of Indian status and degree of blood.

As the law now stands, the establishment of Indian status depends largely on existing tribal enrollments. Naturally, those tribes who have continued to maintain their status as political entities and whose members have continued to enroll their children have no difficulties. Since even federally unrecognized tribes have continued to maintain their internal governments, their enrollments are considered valid. Unregistered descendants of a federally recognized tribe may establish this status if they can prove that they are the legal descendants of one or more grandparents enrolled in that tribe. That is, they may be as little as one quarter of blood quantum. This does not automatically make them full members; that would be a matter of tribal decision. It does, however, establish their eligibility for a number of programs.

The unregistered descendants of unrecognized tribes must establish that at least one parent was enrolled and thus that they are one-half Indian.

With this absolute necessity of establishing some rule of order, it is almost certain that there are a lot of Indians out there somewhere that *nobody* recognizes. Expecting nothing and getting nothing, they are Indian by preference with nothing to do but contemplate the memories of their people. Wouldn't it be strange if, in the dark loneliness of their separation, they would stumble on the truth about the history of their race?

These, too, we must bring, that there may be one fold—and one Shepherd.

CHAPTER II

The White Suitcase

I am becoming known as the belle of the Greyhound bus. No matter how many times I vow to return to my snug little corner, all anyone has to do is brandish a ticket and I'm off again.

Planes are quicker; a bus is crowded and you are stuck for hours with your feet asleep and someone's elbow in your ribs. A bus is life in the raw with upholstered seats.

I like to travel by bus.

There is no better way, according to those of us who believe in signs, to see and learn so much about the country and the people who live here. The scenery is more diverse than one could possibly see by car, for the conveyance plunges into narrow alleyways and underground canyons one would otherwise certainly miss.

The people—oh, what a cross section of humanity of every size and shape and color! Japanese tourists with sophisticated cameras slung about their necks. Retired farmers returning from chasing dreams in California to the welcome sight of Indiana pastures. Young people on holiday shouldering backpacks to trek off into some far wilderness. Once I met two elderly schoolteachers from London seeing the "American Rockies" for the first time...and a honeymoon couple from Switzerland awed by the barren grandeur of our western mountains.

I have learned that in some cities I do not ask questions—even of those who are paid to answer. There is a look of sudden fear as though I might be carrying a concealed weapon. A driver through a lonely stretch of country apologizes for stopping now and then, saying he is the "local paper boy." Rest stops are antiseptic clean and barren, paper-strewn and filthy, or plush and softly lit havens; but always there's variety.

There is one piece of equipment I worry most about—an oversized white bag that holds my papers. No one could fail to be impressed when lifting it, for its weight might well indicate that it holds half the Fort Knox gold. Envisioning lawsuits for strained backs I always try to warn the baggage people. Once, in the bustle of arrival, I failed to speak quickly enough and a hard-pressed baggage man reached for the white case on the run. The bag stayed put and he didn't. His legs continued to run and his arms flailed as he cavorted to maintain his balance. He looked at me reproachfully, "You might have warned me!" And once in Canada, where there were no baggage carriers at all, a bus driver six feet tall and inches more took pity on me and *ran* the full length of the terminal with the weighty thing—a feat which to my mind should qualify him for the Olympics.

The white case holds my papers: bales of fact sheets on Indian affairs, my collection of copy books in which I am always going to write a book, a tape recorder (seldom used), and perhaps six or eight books from friends who know my passion for reading.

As it has turned out, very few pieces of this equipment are ever taken from the suitcase, but it looks so *professional* to ascend a podium with my arms full of extra ammunition!

Actually, the white suitcase is a relative newcomer to my family of baggage. It had a predecessor—a lightweight thing of no particular value except the full length zipper which made it convenient when I occasionally wanted to look inside. The demise of the zipper case was a tragicomedy of errors, the acquisition of the white case a time of great personal loss.

The zipper case was with me while I went tooling up and down Michigan from Mt. Pleasant to the Straits of Mackinac and across the Upper Peninsula. At Grayling I slid it far under my bed lest I be tempted to study while I reveled in the beauties of Edgewater-on-the-Au Sable—surely the most delightful fishing camp in the world. Even those who go there only to fish find it impressive; for the lovely, weathered log cabins stand no more than a half dozen yards from the river. Since it was also the home of dear friends, I was privileged to view it from another angle. The comfortable farmhouse—not just restored but improved—boasted a tiny office in the front hallway; but I could not stop for that. I caught a glint of the sun on water and, in hypnotic trance wandered past the antique dining table, the deep couches, and hove to with my eyes smack dab against the biggest window in the world. Just beyond, the Au Sable chuckled darkly from its wooded banks.

Here I donned buckskins and moccasins—oh, the lovely feel of moccasins on woodland grasses! Snapshots of a "real Indian" in the untrammeled wilderness revealed the truth about what kind of an Indian *I* am when I stepped clumsily into my first canoe. But oh, the delicious realization that I could shed civilization like taking off a glove to glide down that whispering river... forever!

Forever was just a day.

Then it was off and away to audiences waiting to hear the great drama—the high, heady tale of a people despised and forgotten who once heard the voice of the Father of all and his promise.

Indian country. Land of birch bark canoes and musical names. Land of Indians getting off their supplicant knees and sitting at the desks of tribal offices. Manpower... Health, Education, and Welfare... *Title IV!*

When, in the course of human events, it becomes apparent that the children of the people grow weary of taunts and refuse to go to school, they can, under the Indian Education Act, Title IV, inaugurate a system on the Reservation. The classrooms may be ill-housed and under-equipped but, by all that is merciful, the children can wake in their own homes in the morning and sleep in their own beds at night.

Near the little town of Gladstone a small band of Menominee struggled to get a school under way. These people were doing very well, for they had one great advantage not provided by the law: they had *spirit.*

We climbed from our car and approached a station wagon loaded with children.

"I hear that you have a school," I said. "Where is it?"

They tumbled out, all eager and full of pride.

"That's it," they cried. "That's *our* school!"

It was a long, low building that might have been put up in a hurry. There were no frills. School was dismissed for the day, but in the tribal office—a cubicle in the heart of the building—the tribal chairman—chair*lady,* if you please—was up to her elbows in papers. Her small son played at her feet.

The conversation was slow to start, for such is the way of the people, but it left no doubt as to the determination and pride of this little community.

"Most people in the town don't even know we exist," our hostess said, "but one thing was plain; our children weren't learning, and we had far too many dropouts. They just hated to go to school. Now we can't keep them in bed in the morning."

When I asked what she thought might have been the difficulty, she was quite frank.

"Well, you know that children can be cruel to each other, and they pick up attitudes from their parents, even when the parents make an effort to conceal the old inherited feelings. People look at our poverty, the tumbledown houses, and maybe the kids don't have the right clothes—I don't know. Here, we don't have to worry about who likes Indians and who doesn't. The students just learn their lessons."

Food for thought!

One of my party asked if the outer community might make more of an effort to get acquainted, perhaps attend some Reservation social. For a moment her eyes flashed as she contemplated tourists looking for beads and feathers. Then she said gently, "Later, maybe, when we have proved to ourselves what we can do. We have a lot of plans...a laundromat, some cleanup work."

I came away full of pride. This, too, is the old Indian way; people prove that they *can*.

It was there—after the kindly congregations, the heartwarming glow that came from reviving our faith through shared witness—that I received a sad phone call from my sister. Our mother had left our world. Peacefully, quietly, and without making a big thing of it, forming with her lips even after there was no voice with which to speak the words "I love you," she had gone into a world where, at least for the moment, we could not follow.

Mamma—of the quick curiosity and the ability to go straight to the heart of a matter—who taught her girls that no matter how things appeared on the surface, they should look for the truth beneath. This incredible woman who went from a lace-trimmed Victorian girlhood to an oxteam in the Canadian Northwest and came in time to commute by jet plane to Hawaii, who had a thousand tales to tell of wolves and white wildernesses and horses with hooves that softened in the marshy turf of Athabasca. Mamma, who listened with absorbed interest to the truths of other faiths—and granted truth to all—but who would "be a Methodist until she died"; who could "let out" furs until they became a soft and silky blanket or turn a hand-me-down into a work of fashion. Mamma, who had that instant intuition and could read between the lines so that I could never hide when things were bad.

My heart was wild with grief! And here I was hundreds of miles from Arizona, where she had spent her last years surrounded by every comfort and rebelling against the constant inroads of age that slowed her hands until she felt inadequate. Here I was—and there would be no way to look once more on that dear face. She was to be cremated, and by the time I arrived there would be—what? A silver urn with the handful of ashes that once enclosed that bright spirit? Nothing? Something? Every fiber of my heritage rose in rebellion. Not to return to the friendly earth? Not to give back to the earth what we have taken in life? How gross! Yet it was said that this was quick and clean, and in that day of resurrection the Great Builder could reconstruct from a handful of ashes or a lump of clay a new body of shining beauty.

Nevertheless, my grief demanded that I rush to join with family in some last tribute to this dear earthly angel. Angel? She would have scoffed at that. There was, however, one theatrical maxim she had preached—words which certainly never came from her strict Victorian-Methodist past, but an ideal firmly entrenched: "The show must go on."

No matter what came or went, once committed to a task, she did it. For me there remained one last talk, so I knew I must push my grief into some tight-closed cubicle and "get on with it." The congregation at Gladstone was patient with a rather distraught witness who rambled up and down and strove to keep that little door completely closed.

The miles across the Upper Peninsula crawled by, then south at last to the haven at Grayling. Here I would pick up the zipper bag, and the first leg of the journey into loss would be over.

Desperate phone calls revealed that there would be no way out of Grayling until the following morning. I made a tearful call to the most efficient of the clan, Diana, in Indianapolis.

"Don't worry, mom; I'll arrange everything and call you back."

Later: "The airlines people had all the information. You'll have to take a bus to Detroit, but you will get the airport bus right at the terminal. You'll fly by Delta and arrive in Indianapolis at 1:30. I'll be there to meet you with our tickets to Phoenix on American Airlines, leaving at 1:55."

I repeated the schedule: bus to Detroit, airport bus, ticket to Indianapolis (no need to cash a check), change to American. Perfectly simple. In a glow of admiration for the efficiency of the airlines, I boarded the bus at 6:30 in the morning and the miles began to unroll.

The terminal at Detroit was a beehive of activity, and the wild-eyed woman dashing about asking questions received uncertain answers. It appeared that there was no airport bus leaving the terminal. The stop was six blocks away at the entrance to a hotel.

Six blocks! I glanced uneasily at the bag (the zipper was beginning to separate and a corner of paper was peeping through). The taxi discharged me and my luggage at the proper corner where I spent agonizing moments shoving papers back into the bag.

The airport was a veritable palace of long marble corridors. Brisk attendants dashed about with luggage carts. We hoisted the zipper case aboard and I trotted alongside, one hand vainly trying to control its bulging contents.

"I have to get some tape!" I yelled.

"That's all right," said the captain of our craft. "First we'll get this to the desk."

Arriving at Delta I found there was not only no reservation in my name but no plane to Indianapolis. The papers crawled out of my demolished bag.

"Try American..." the desk clerk said.

"My bag!" I gasped.

Oh, knight of the red cap with a luggage cart for a charger! My hero grabbed a roll of tape from the desk and literally swathed that bag with bandages. It emerged a neat parcel with the papers blissfully confined. We zoomed the full length of the airport where American Airlines confirmed my reservation to Indianapolis. I tumbled aboard.

In Indianapolis I came boiling into the terminal. No Diana! I dashed hither and yon, then stood uncertainly.

The luggage...it would have to be transferred to another plane. I tore through the endless miles of corridor and stopped in horror. According to the clock I had ten minutes to launch!

A sign over a doorway said "baggage-master" and I blurted out the disjointed tale to a sleepy figure behind the desk.

"Don't worry," I heard for the umpteenth time. "We'll take care of it. You go on back to American and look for your daughter."

Still no Diana!

I approached the dignified individual who controlled the entrance to the wild blue yonder.

"Oh, yes," he said. "You're confirmed on 457 leaving in five minutes."

The very plane from which I had just disembarked! How could everyone be so infernally calm?

"Your daughter's probably on board," he added. "She's been looking for you."

"I have no ticket," I said feebly.

"Oh, she has the tickets," he returned happily. He opened the gate and I was somehow aboard, without ticket, without boarding pass, without my wits.

Diana was *not* on board. She was at the Delta window throwing the tantrum of the ages.

"We're sorry," the attendant was saying, "but it was probably Allegheny's fault."

I sank wearily into a seat and wondered if I would be thrown off in midair. Suddenly, one minute before takeoff, there was Diana coming triumphantly down the aisle, waving the tickets.

Out of chaos into calm!

* * *

The chapel was a funeral director's dream of lush carpets and soft music piped from an unseen source.

Emptiness and quiet—not a footstep, not a whisper disturbed the silence. There was no flower-draped coffin filled with precious burden, no silver urn...only a picture framed in flowers.

Those few of her family left to join in this last farewell stood about uneasily. We had been uncertain what to do about flowers; a vase here and there seemed lost in that vast cavern. There had been many gifts in her name to various good works, a much more lasting tribute than fading wreaths. Still—"It's terribly empty," said my sister.

Old rites, barbaric though they might have been, by their very familiarity carried a family through those first difficult hours of loss. I longed for the comfort of Indian voices singing the night away, bearing on wings of song this precious soul to Paradise.

Then the last, heartrending task of packing and disposing of our mother's few possessions. We approached the deed with misgivings. Mamma had taught us above all to value the privacy of other people's things. Suddenly we were struck with a new grief. This woman—this blessed woman who had given of herself for ninety-three loving years—had almost nothing.

She had never owned a car. The few pieces of furniture she had once acquired had long ago been given away. Surrounded in her last years by every comfort, every loving care in my sister's home, she left an inventory of three items:

A French china clock of uncertain vintage but holding memories of another age; this would remain in my sister's home.

The forget-me-not blue tea set, said to be at least two hundred years old, would pass into my keeping but— with my constant journeys—would be entrusted to my daughter.

Her well-worn Bible would be bestowed on the one grandson who had remained a Methodist.

That was all, except for a few items she had been making for Christmas presents while the once-keen eyes were fading...precious things to go to grandchildren and friends. Yet she was no sober-faced ascetic. She adored pretty clothes...but she never wore them out; garments I had seen ten years ago hung fresh and neat in the press.

"Isn't there something else you'd like to have?" my sister asked.

I looked about. In the wide closet I saw a blur of white through tears. The white suitcase that had traveled with her in happier times, the case that had held not only personal items but, invariably, gifts for everyone including candy for the children.

So the white suitcase now travels from coast to coast with me, sturdily bearing the increasing burden of papers which contain the hopes and dreams and agonies of Indian people.

And to me it bears witness of a life well-spent—the memory of my mother.

CHAPTER 12

Indian—and Christian

Possibly the subject which causes most discomfort among Indians is the breach between Christians and followers of the various tribal religions known as Traditionalists. An understanding of the basic tenets of these traditional beliefs reveals them to be highly ethical, demanding rigid standards of conduct and honor. The time-honored rituals have sustained a people through centuries of difficult circumstances. As the various nations begin to regain their pride and self-sufficiency, it is natural that there should be a renewed interest in the ancient religious practice.

Yet there are many Christian Indians, and probably many more, who are torn between the desire to accept Christ and a reluctance to embrace a faith different from that of their brothers. The effect is a sad one, for we tend not to discuss our private inclinations unless we are very sure they are shared by the one to whom we are talking. This is a sorry state of affairs among people whose tradition ordered that they should "speak often of the Great Spirit, to the children and to the strangers among us."

Frequently it is difficult to persuade the two factions to attend the same meetings to discuss community problems. Each is fearful of offending the other, and they tiptoe around the subject, becoming ever more isolated. This is not traditionally Indian; it certainly is not Christian.

It is important that we first understand the reason for this strange state of affairs. What is it among Indians that makes a conversion to Christianity such a traumatic experience? What can be done to heal this grievous wound? The answers to both questions lie deep in tradition. Perhaps only by looking with clear eyes at all that occurred in Indian history can we bridge this gap of misunderstanding.

We are becoming aware that, as the Indian has long claimed, there were seven great "races" of people among the ancients. We cannot as yet identify these ancestral roots, nor can we establish whether they were, indeed, separate races, separate nations, or simply diverse cultures. For the purpose of study, historians have designated them as language groups.

When the first white settlers arrived, some six hundred languages were spoken by tribes across the land. Though many of them were obviously of common ancestry, it was sometimes difficult to find sufficient common root words to assign them to a definite language group.

The picture that emerged at an early date, and has persisted in some degree until very recent times, was that of a vast miscellany of tribal groups, each with its own language, custom, mode of dress, and its own religion. It was, in fact, this distinctive religious concept that provided a tribe's self-image. There simply was no argument; thus-and-so was the way of the tribal entity.

Underlying the distinctive ritual form, of course,

might be concepts held in common with other faiths. Thus, in the last analysis, Indians were monotheistic, though they recognized certain "elemental figures" as assistants to the Great Spirit. These elementals occupied a place similar to the saints in the Roman Catholic Church. They were intercessors, or were given charge over certain aspects of creation. They were to be respected but not adored.

Each tribal religion seemed to emphasize some one particular facet of relationship with the Creator. It is almost as though to each group had been given one piece of a giant puzzle which it attempted to preserve in purity. One might concentrate on the gifts of medicine and healing, as in the Midewi religion of the Algonquin; another might be caught up in the spiritual nature of all creation as in the Orenda concept of the Iroquois.

We begin to understand the importance of this identification with a tribal religion when we realize that in the creation stories of the various cultures the Great Spirit was credited with the creation of the earth, but when it came to the human race, he created the particular tribe of which one was a member as the apex of his achievement.

Consequently, the various names by which the tribes identified themselves did not translate as "the people" as has been commonly supposed, but as "people" which is an altogether different idea. The Leni-Lenape, or Delaware, were "real men," the Ho-de-nau-soh-ne or Iroquois, "real humans," and so forth. The implication was that they recognized the existence of other beings with the requisite number of arms and legs, but they alone were the genuine human beings.

This is one difference between Indian converts and those from other religions. A Catholic may become a Protestant; a Jew may even become a Christian; there may be great sorrow on the part of relatives, or there may be ostracism, but they are still "human." The Indians of the various tribes were not so sure. Though not put into so many words, a residue of this feeling is still present in the unease that exists between Christian and Traditionalist Indians.

This also is the background for the idea that Indian religion cannot be separated from Indian social or political life. Traditions and rituals established a person's identity as a "human" creature.

There are, naturally, other opposing concepts to make a missionary's task difficult. Even a superficial examination of these will give some idea of the gulf an Indian must cross in becoming a Christian. These few are offered not to extol the virtues of one or the other but simply to point up the differences in ideology among people who are all—Christian and Traditionalist—trying to do the same thing: please their heavenly Father.

Take prayer: Christians drop to their knees and bow their head in submission to the Master's will. Humility before God and reverence impel them to this action. Indians stand with uplifted head before their Maker. This attitude says, "Here I stand, revealed to my Creator. If there be any flaw, any ugliness, let him find it and bring me into harmony with his plan."

Consider stewardship: Christians are impelled to translate their love for Jesus Christ into some aspect of social service. At great sacrifice of time and money, they want to reach out in their own communities—or to people they will never see.

Indians know about social responsibility. Their first obligation is to take care of their families. This, however, includes not just parents and children, but a brother's children and grandchildren, the wife's sister's children, cousins, and the great extended family of which they are a part. Such obligation involves not just filling in the gaps economically but in giving of time and talents; nor does the responsibility carry the rider, "if you can."

Even at this time, after the protest movements of the 60s and 70s exposed the impoverished conditions in Indian communities, the individual Indian is often loath to admit personal poverty, for it reflects on one's ability to perform this social obligation. The Indian cannot "reach out" without depriving at least some of these relationships ordained by the Creator. To do so constitutes a bid for public approval.

The other great area of contention lies in the importance of church structures in the Christian community. Few Indians become excited about the building of church edifices. Based on the concept that the Great Spirit made the world and made it beautiful, it is difficult for Indians to conceive that improvement be made on the design by piling up stone and concrete. While they may see the wisdom of some protection from the elements so they may continue to worship in the cold of winter, they find it an alien thought that God should need an edifice or house.

These are some of the conflicting areas of concept that have underlain the tragic division between Traditionalist Indians and Christian Indians. It is my belief that this breach can be closed and that many who have been torn by the desire to follow Christ and the fear of separation from their people may find that they can, indeed, be Christian and Indian as well. There is, in fact, a new term coming into use—Christian Traditionalist—and it just may be the impetus for the bridge that will reunite the two groups.

Tragic mistakes have been made by Christians, both missionaries and lay people. It would be well to air them here before any attempt to bind up the wounds is made. Seen in black and white, these ideas are as offensive to Christians as they have been to the Indian. Many of the experiences of Indians with Christian doctrines in the past have included one or more of these demeaning ideas:

We don't want to hear about your old beliefs. They are evil. Put them away.

Your grandfathers haven't a hope of heaven since they did not join a Christian church (usually a specific doctrine).

Get these children out of their homes and away from all this culture business.

Indians are dark, therefore they must be accursed.

Indians are poor, dirty, backward; therefore they must be less favored. Let them get out and be like the rest of us, and in time they shall be saved.

We look around and see that the thirst for power and material wealth has polluted the skies, poisoned the water, laid waste the forests that drank up the annual flood, and covered the choicest agricultural areas with concrete; for us all of these aspects of creation constitute the property of the Great Spirit. We hear the statistics of ever-increasing crime, mental illness, abortion (a heinous sin in Indian religion), and the breakdown of family life...yet we are told that America is predominantly Christian.

Since Indian religious and civic life overlap, we often tend to judge Christian standards by our experiences with the political; and our conclusions are certainly not true of all our Christian brothers.

"They [the white men] are greedy." It is a common belief that all white men subscribe to the doctrine of manifest destiny—that they do not care, or do not care *enough,* about their neighbor's needs.

"This civilization is built on competition; the push to be more, get more, hold more than the other fellow."

Indians are not competitive, a fact that has at last caught on with educators. We may strive to do better than before, but we simply do not care and are, in fact, embarrassed by the thought of trying to outdo others.

These are ugly ideas when we see them in print, and we each disclaim any guilt of such thoughts. They have been present, nevertheless, and must be cleansed before the healing can begin.

Having now exposed the wound, we may proceed to heal this controversy that exists between these "children of one Father." We must begin with the same ancient point we chose in tracing this division.

A whole new science of linguistics known as glottochronology has emerged. The principle underlying this complexity of syllables is that, separated from the root or parent stock, a language loses a measurable number of words within a given length of time. Having established a table of measurements, the linguist is able to give a rough approximation of the time at which a tribe separated from the original stock. It has also been possible through this study to define the protolangauge of widely separated tribal groups.

What this is going to mean, in simple terms, is that many more relationships will be recognized by Indians than they were wont to acknowledge. The original parent stocks embraced seven...possibly eight...language groups which calls to mind the idea of "seven races." As this becomes fully apparent, Indians will take one more step toward "the wisdom of their fathers," one more step toward the enlarging of their horizon of memories as they begin to draw closer together within the original nations. The giant puzzle with its many pieces—spirit, earth, fire, water, healing—may again be one faith.

They may even remember that in the dim legends of the past, ancient ancestors paid reverence to the Prince of Heaven, Lord of the Dawn Star, who once visited the children of the earth.

They may remember and recognize many truths of the scriptures as having been a part of the ancient tradition. They may even cause more established Christians to take a new look at this Jesus whom they wish to follow. Seen through the eyes of these newly wakened children of the kingdom, the truths he taught may truly change the world.

There is an old story told in our family of an ancestor who was converted—but for a reason the missionaries of his day would have found strange, if not a trifle amusing.

Senoughleea was an Oneida whose career spanned a period of at least forty-four years. He must have been a young man when he signed the Treaty of Fort Stanwix in 1795, for according to family tradition he was one of the party that migrated to Ontario in 1840. Some time during the intervening years he obviously was exposed to the Old Testament scriptures, for he became convinced that this book, now revered by the white people, had once belonged to Indian people. He found many parallels between the laws of the ancient Israelites and the time-honored customs of his own people. In fact, as the years went by he was known to voice his bitterness that this was apparently one more thing the paleface had confiscated, though he was uncertain as to how or when this had occurred. The great dream of his life was that someday, with formal ceremony, the ancient record would be returned to those to whom it had once belonged. He must have been a great trial to the Christian missionaries.

To European settlers, who brought the scriptures with them, the idea of the birth of the Son of God in a place called Palestine seems not to have occasioned any disorientation. The long history preceding their migration from their native lands had brought their ancestors step by traceable step from ancient peoples. Egypt, Greece, Babylon, Rome, and Palestine were known to them. The conditions of great empires, national boundaries, and successions of rulers were things they had experienced. All of these conditions the Indian viewed with suspicion and distrust. These were alien and indeed frightening concepts to the Indian, as they were to many peoples of the world. It is not strange that Christianity became popularly known as "the white man's religion," for none of these conditions had any significance to the Indian in that period of his history. Also, since the spread of the gospel went hand in hand with the misery engendered by conquest, obviously Jesus Christ must be the "totem" of white people, their own particular god of protection and power.

Was there any way in which this sad misunderstanding could have been avoided? Probably not, at that time; the whole of humankind had to mount a higher step to an understanding of the preciousness of other cultures. Once this happens, there are many ways in which the truths known to those of good will may meet.

If, as an Indian, I read the scriptures without stopping to consider that they came to us through the hands of those who were, after all, our enemies, I can—like Senoughleea—find many parallels in our own traditions. I find that, first of all, they are the account of ancient people and their relationship with their God. When they departed from him and his laws they were afflicted with many troubles. When they returned to him and worshiped him as their Creator, their lives were peaceful and productive. There is nothing strange or unique about this. In all our traditions we acknowledge the Supreme Being, Creator of heaven and earth—though we have always thought that the terms "the Great Spirit" or the "First Great Cause" more perfectly describe the nature of the Creator spoken of in the scriptures as Jehovah than does the word "God."

If we examine the creation stories of our various nations and compare them with the book of Genesis, we find that all ascribe creation to a great intelligence or spirit who was the author of the earth and all that ever existed or ever will exist. Many of our legends simply go into greater detail about the way in which creation proceeded than does the brief account in the book of Genesis, but in essence all are saying the same thing; we acknowledge the omnipotence of the Great One as the author and director of our being, who is indeed the eternal Father of all creation throughout all the world. To imply that he created only the world of Israel, or only the world of the Indian, is to limit his boundless power and to diminish him.

There should be nothing threatening to anyone's personal relationships with God in hearing the many experiences these ancient people had. They are very much like the tales we told around our campfires—tales of migrations, of quarrels between brothers, of the misery of a people under great persecution—and they assert overall the truths we learned in our history. Perhaps we should not dismiss too lightly the experiences of other peoples, for the moral truths beneath the words were apparently given to all who lived on the earth in some far time. "Thou shalt not take the name of God in vain...Thou shalt not steal...or bear false witness"—these are such a basic, ingrained part of our conscience that even if we fall far short of the ideal we recognize them, whatever our faith.

I find as well, in the pages of this ancient book, the customs which so impressed that great-grandfather.

Here are the Cities of Refuge, an idea familiar to our fathers; laws governing the separation of women during lunar cycles and after childbirth; burnt offerings and the Feast of Atonement (in which Indians substituted an unblemished white dog); the laws governing the treatment of strangers... the list goes on and on. Thus, apparently, the Old Testament should present no problems.

It is in the New Testament that we stumble; yet, if we had had the full story, our reception of it might have been quite different. For, as we come to the New Testament era, we find a time torn by violence, strife, and greed—very much like our times today. The only difference, of course, is that those conditions can now be multiplied by faster travel, more subtle interpretations of the law (with consequently more loopholes), and more people. Still there was a nation under the conqueror's heel. There was a nation losing its last hope of any redress; its holy places despoiled and defiled, the lives of its people in constant jeopardy.

Into that time appeared a great teacher—one who lived very simply but who by his life proved that faith can be kept with God despite surrounding sin and corruption. He lived as a man among them, not as a God far removed from human temptation. That, it would seem, ought to have been enough to make his life effective. He and his followers, however, claimed that he was the Son of God, and that was a startling claim—one that would take some marvelous manifestations to sustain. It is very difficult for any human being to allow one who is seemingly another man to make such a claim. This is where human arrogance and limited vision step in to substitute personal conceit for the Universal Spirit. It is not, as the unbelievers say, that humans created a god, but that they strive to limit God, to make him behave according to their own feeble understanding.

If Jesus *was* the Son of God, the Universal Creator, then he must have been sent to all the scattered peoples of the world. Many doctrines have maintained, in effect, that because of the limitation of the length of time he was to spend on earth he commissioned his disciples to travel to all the world delivering his message. At the same time they attempted to say that death itself could not chain him. Something was wrong: either he *was* the Son of God, and neither time nor space could limit him, or he was simply a man, limited as are the rest of us. Or perhaps something was left out of the story, or our own limited understanding closed our ears. Something *was* missing.

To say that Jesus commissioned his disciples to carry his message where he could not go not only demoted him from his divine position but opened the way for a multitude of people to make capital of this directive. It provided for the founding of complicated organizations requiring vast sums collected from impoverished people eager to do as, it was said, the Master wished. It paved the way for generations of conquerors to grind and destroy in the name of Christ. It encouraged the building of great temples and cathedrals, while the simple people that the Master loved existed in poverty and despair. Nothing in his words and life in that far land and time would indicate his approval of such a situation.

What *did* Jesus require of his followers in that mideastern world?

They were to bear witness to the things they had seen and heard even in peril of their lives and freedom. They were to testify that in the message of Jesus was a declaration of such love that in responding to it, people would find within themselves a portion of the heavenly

Spirit that would enable them to do good and not evil. They were to take this witness into "all the world," but because they were quite human that directive meant the world as they knew it. Their journeys covered great distances according to the transportation of the time, but they hardly covered all the world as it was known to the Creator. This should not detract from the importance of their task. There is revealed in their service to God the highest nobility to which they could aspire, for they literally put their lives on the line for the truth they had witnessed. There had been revealed to them the *clear channel to the Eternal Spirit* that had been sought throughout the earth since the dawn of time. That channel was this incarnation of the Logos, the Word, which had been with God at the creation—the divine entity through which the material creation had emerged and through which it must return. (Incidentally this is a very acceptable concept to Indians.)

Born as a child in a place so full of hate and brutal power, Jesus demonstrated that righteousness does not depend on material wealth or principalities or powers or anything save love—that word of which we are most afraid and which is the final, eternal verity, inviolate and indestructable.

It is not difficult to believe in Jesus as a man or as a great teacher or to see in his teachings the ideals by which we ought to live. The specific difference in this new revelation is the acceptance of the divinity of the Cristos, the Anointed—the recognition of a power above and beyond human control or manipulation, and the beautiful truth that this channel of love is forever open to the heavenly Father in this world and the next. What a world we would have if we could finally accept this truth—for all of us, as human creatures caught in the tide of earthly confusion, long for something outside ourselves, some way of making sense of life. Like fish impelled to return to their spawning grounds, we have an instinctive hunger—a sense of something missing—and the channel is open to all who truly abide by the law of love ordained from the beginning. The sins of pride, greed, and lust for power block the passage. The teachings of Jesus rule out the validity of "manifest destiny" as it has been interpreted. It is our manifest destiny to regain the spirituality in which we were created.

One thing became apparent: this truth could not be bludgeoned into being by any organization or legislated by any earthly government. It had nothing to do with forms of ritual or architectural styles of churches—and no one or any group had a corner on the Father's love. It was at this particular point that humans began to stray from this truth of Jesus Christ; for out of this revelation of God to his children grew mighty organizations that increased in power until they ceased to be the instruments of the kingdom and became human instruments instead.

How, then, was the story of God's love to be carried throughout the world if not by conquest? Jesus gave the answer, but it was seldom mentioned except in passing. Only one brief line revealed this mystery, but how could there be more? Those ancient scribes were recording what they actually saw and heard in their own land. He said, "Other sheep I have, not of this fold. I go to them."

Perhaps if more attention had been paid to that one brief statement, the acceptance of Christ as the Son of God might have been accomplished long ago and without all the bloodshed. For, if it was acknowledged that he had other sheep and was going to them, it implied that he knew of all the scattered peoples of the world. If so, he knew what other men of his time did not. We are now aware that while these things were taking place in Palestine, cities were being built in Central and South America. Great colonies of people moved out from those cultures. The islands of the sea were peopled; the world, in fact, was filled with those who claimed one Father of creation. Yet they were unknown to the mideastern world.

Is there any evidence of such a visitor in other places? Yes! And the evidence grows as more and more the curtains of the past are drawn apart by scattered people. The Polynesians pay great reverence to the God Wakea, who appeared and lived among them for a brief period many centuries before the first white man landed. The lessons he taught are hauntingly familiar:

That which you would not that others should do to you, do not to them.
Love your brother. Honor your parents and the aged among you.
Live with simple faith that your heavenly Father will sustain you.

In the land southward the story is told of the visitation of the Son of Heaven, Lord of Dawn. He had power over the winds and over the water. And the truths *he* taught are hauntingly familiar. Beyond this, his followers say that he had been born of a virgin mother in a far country, that he had been killed upon a tree by his enemies, and then had come to their people in his original godly form. In fact, terrible cruelties were inflicted on the peoples of Central America by the Spanish because, they said, "These savages were deluded by the devil into thinking they had been visited by the Son of God." Because these people dared suggest he had taught them rituals of baptism and a type of communion with him, the arrogant conquerors directed they be torn and mutilated. This is historical truth.

Only when faced with the mystery of this worldwide

advent of the Son of God do we come face to face with a power greater than our human minds can understand. When this truth is recognized, it will be known that all the earth has received the law of peace and love brought by the Son of heaven. In this Christ (by whatever name throughout the world the languages of his followers distinguished him) who taught the simple laws of love and faith and forgiveness, Indians should well be able to believe. And it is the witness of those who were among the "other sheep of the pasture" which fully defined his limitless power as the one who was "with God" at creation.

In the Iroquois creation story, when the Creator completed all his work—knowing the nature of his people and how easily they might be swayed by things of darkness—he predicted thus:

> Sometime it may again come to pass that you will forget love of persons and of peace. Then I will send another who will aid you dwelling on the earth. Only twice will it be repeated that I will send one to aid you in mind so that you may continue to live.

The followers of Wovoka, in the Ghost Dance Religion, believed in and yearned for the return of the Rejuvenator who would bring a time of peace and renewal and reunion with those who were lost. Whole nations of people counted the centuries and lost their lives because of their faith in the return of Quetzalcoatl. Even so does the Christian believe that One once was sent in a time of great need who will come again to heal the wounds, to break the chains of ignorance and avarice, and to set free those who are bound in spirit.

When, if ever, we can grasp this truth that a universal Father cared enough about his children over all the earth to reveal his truth to them, and that the praise of all his people is precious to him, we shall be free to worship him in spirit and in truth. The Tree of Life deep rooted in these scattered seeds will once again begin to grow and flourish on the earth.

For this is truth:

Jehovah, Yahweh, the Great Spirit, God—call him what we will—is one God and his messenger and Son—call him Jesus, Sega[n] hedus, Quetzalcoatl, Thunderbird, or Fair Wakea—all are one.

CHAPTER 13

Fourteen—with Love

The rules of general conversation seem to decree that sooner or later the subject of children comes up. This always makes me very happy, for though other people may have vastly superior talents or have been involved in a greater number of worthy causes, *I have more kids!*

When I am asked how many children I have, I answer with titillating joy, "Fourteen." It invariably brings forth a gasp of some kind—horror, admiration, or disapproval. There was a time when it was considered a major victory to have made such a contribution to society. Now that there is a population explosion, of course, I am conscious of having boosted the statistics to an alarming degree, as projected into the third or fourth generation.

When it becomes plain that I have helped to produce not just quantity but quality, however, everyone assumes that I am an expert on childrearing or have some magic formula for success. I want to state at the outset that such is not the case. The only wisdom I have gained from such prolonged education is what any parent learns along the way: children, like Rome, aren't built in a day.

There are no magic formulae, because no two children are totally alike—for which I thank heaven! Any two of them presenting the same problems would be just too much. No one has to have fourteen chldren to learn this; it can be discovered with one or two or with none by teaching school or acting as den mother.

I learned one other thing, and I consider this the single most important piece of wisdom granted me—second only to the good news of the gospel. Only two qualities are needed to rear a child: love and common sense, in that order. Notice that I do not include income, adequate housing, nutrition, superior schools, good ministry, or any of the other things that people press so avidly to gain. These are important, of course, and they certainly make the job easier, yet children really need very little of what adults consider essential. What they must have is love; it is as essential to them as sun and rain are to a plant. It always seemed to me a bit like first seeking the kingdom of God—first love, then all the rest will fall into place.

Few of my children remember that there was a Thanksgiving dinner which consisted only of a bowl of potatoes and, as a special treat, a carton of sour cream. Neither do they remember one dinner, Thanksgiving or otherwise, when the ingredient of love was absent. No one was ever rushed from the table to clear the field for a bridge game or other adult pursuit. No conversation was hurried or pushed aside, for each was eager to share the others' developing interests.

I recall the morning that Daniel announced at breakfast, "God made the world in six days—zap!" snapping his young fingers.

Now his father could have let it go at that, for he was

perfectly familiar with the book of Genesis and fully accepted the omnipotence of the Creator. Instead, he grumbled a little dubiously, "That seems like a rather careless way to make a world. We'll talk about it."

And talk about it we did! Out in the yard to visit the bees and hear their marvelous story; into the garden to examine the new springing plants. Lying on our backs to feel the warmth of the sun on our faces while we examined the intricate marvels of all the leaves and grasses.

When their father was through with it, the children had learned several important lessons. They had seen firsthand the evidence of a Creator who had not only ordained the earth and the passing seasons, but who had created life that continually renews itself. How wonderful it was to know not only that God was concerned with making big things like mountains but that he had fashioned the delicate mosses at their feet. The children became aware, too, that their lives were like the growth of leaves and would eventually come into the fullness of seedtime, according to the design in God's plan. This was fairly heavy stuff for children and, of course, they were not aware of the philosophy or of the terms. What they had had was the first lesson in the preciousness of life.

This is the particular kind of love I think is essential in rearing a child. It is not a love that leads simply to patting a head or rocking a child to sleep—though both are part of it. Nor, certainly, is it a permissive love that leads parents to excuse naughtiness. It is a love that is truly eager to listen, never too busy to share in wakening consciousness.

I am deeply aware that the whole situation was different for us than for most families. The children's father did his work at home, so he was always on the scene. He was often under great pressure for time, for providing even the necessities for such a houseful was like pouring water down a well. The little ones would make frequent and unscheduled appearances at his side, bearing some small gift. A tiny stone, a few seeds rolled in bits of newspaper would be offered, and childish voices would chorus "Happy Birthday!" as they had chanted last week and would chant tomorrow. He would lay down his tools, encircle them with his arms, and together they would examine the proffered treasures.

I refer primarily to the children's relationship with their father, because it was of special significance. Although they lost his presence at a time when his companionship would have meant a lot to them, his influence never faded.

Their first assurance of security came at their father's hands. We "wrapped" our infants. By this I mean that whenever the baby began to cry, though we knew it was dry and fed, we folded a blanket into a firm pad; the little limbs were brought straight and a blanket was firmly wrapped so that the child was held in a close cocoon. The idea behind this was the old-fashioned recognition that an infant has come from a place where he was close and warm. The new world was full of space and insecurity. He had no control over his hands, and those little fists coming out of nowhere to hit at his face were frightening. Be that as it may, the child would immediately become quiet. Solemn eyes would take one look at the safe world and close in sleep.

My husband usually performed this chore for no particular reason other than that he could do it better than I. Later, when the child awoke, the blankets would be unfolded and there would be much stretching and crowing...but no tears.

When Dan, in college, applied for an R.O.T.C. scholarship, he had to face a panel of officers and impress them with his worth. One of the questions he was asked was, "Who is the person above all others you would take as a pattern for your life?" His major told me later that every other applicant had named some great military leader or figure of history. Dan's answer was "My father."

Of course, I came in somewhere along there and, though the details escape me, it must have been as natural as breathing for children are not fooled, and our children today are as confident of my love as they are in the return of spring. I do recall one time when we were displaying our leather at a craft show. Two ladies leaned across my table and whispered, "We don't want the children to hear this, but we think they are wonderful young people." What I remember is my surprise that it should be treated as some dark secret. I answered more loudly than was perhaps necessary.

"Of course! I know it, and I tell them so every day of their lives." (They were not "wonderful" every day of their lives, but it gave them something to live up to.)

To me this love ingredient poured out to children becomes as sounding brass and tinkling cymbals if it is not buttressed and underpinned by parents' love of one another. I don't suppose any of the children would be able, even today, to describe how, when, or why they were aware that their father and mother not only loved each other but were, in fact, in love. This is another thing about which I have a great humility. In this present society it is not always possible to erect the defenses that keep two human beings within the fortress of their love for one another; but they should try, not just for the sake of the children but because something beautiful can grow out of the extra effort of understanding.

We were never particularly demonstrative in our caring for each other. Both of us had come from backgrounds where adult manifestations of affection were strictly private affairs. It would have been rather difficult anyhow. It's virtually impossible to embrace separated by fourteen children occupied with their various pursuits. Our love was manifested by our regard for one another. If a taxi pulled up to the door to deliver a sheaf of 'mums bought by their father from a flower cart, it was no great surprise. He loved their mother. If mother rushed to the door when he came home, it wasn't to bring in the groceries. She loved their father and was as eager as they for that first sight of him.

It was manifested, too, in the particular role we each occupied in the life of the family. Dad was the captain; I was the first lieutenant. This implied that even he had a superior officer, but in this particular army there was going to be no discrepancy in command.

They well knew that people could have vast differences of opinion and still love each other. They heard us argue mightily on such matters as world affairs or the comparative virtues of Arabian and Morgan horses. They never heard us argue about questions of discipline or proposed legislation in the family. These we threshed out in the privacy of the bedroom. Once all reports, suggestions, budget, primary rules, and personal inclinations had been considered, we presented a united front. This actually came under the heading of common sense. If we had ever allowed any of our children the luxury of playing one parent against the other, we would have been swamped.

"Free expression" meant that each hope, dream, and talent was important, and every consideration would be given to help in bringing hopes to fulfillment. Absolutely never did whining, screaming, wheedling, or throwing a tantrum bring the desired result.

It has always seemed to me unfair to allow children to grow up totally undisciplined and unrestricted in their demands, then thrust them into a world that doesn't care whether they have their candy or not.

Such laws as we had were overall standards which held fast. Absolute honesty and a regard for property were first on the list. And that meant the pennies under the rug as well as those in mother's purse, the neighbor's strawberries as well as the school windows.

Household rules were firm but could on occasion be relaxed. It was a rule that every child had to be in his place, scrubbed and tidy for mealtimes. No one was going to chase off in fourteen different directions when it was time to eat. As they became involved in school or community activities, however, they were entitled to late meals. Raiding the refrigerator was strictly taboo; and if I sometimes felt a twinge of guilt over this restriction, my guilt was tempered by the thought of twenty-eight hot little hands invading the sanctity of the next meal. The dividend was fourteen lusty appetites three times a day.

Rewards were not given for work done in the house or yard. I am still not sure that this was the best way; I only know it worked for us. It did reinforce the fact that these tasks were the responsibility of all for the upkeep of the home. Money was something earned as a result of skill or service "on the outside." There were blackberries to be picked and sold; beaded necklaces to be made and sold at a craft show, snow to be shoveled. The world was full of opportunity. The trash remained to be taken out, dishes had to be washed and floors swept. The children shared in the production of these unpleasantries, and they had to share in the results.

They knew to the last penny our expenses, and they knew to the last hour how many wallets or beaded earrings it would take to meet them.

Right here this whole exposé of any supposed wisdom on my part is going to disintegrate. I'm talking about a time when three wallets a month paid the rent, and three pairs of earrings fed the crew for a day. I don't think even a parent could compute the income-expense equivalent today. The point I am stumblingly trying to make is that children, in simple common sense, should be brought to realize some of the basic facts of life. They are better off if they know from the beginning that in the very nature of things there will always be some "authority"—whether it be a parent, a teacher, the law, or a top sergeant. It is common sense, also, for a child to learn that money is a perishable commodity, to be used toward the best possible results; but he or she must also recognize its limits. Children who have every wish fulfilled are going to have a terrible shock when they finally operate on their own income.

If these rules seem harsh, let it be noted that we exercised the same control over ourselves as parents. We were not tolerant of any insolence on the part of our children, but neither did we use insulting language to each other...or to them.

Over everything else, of course, was the love of God in our lives. It wasn't necessary to put up any signs; we were aware every moment of every day that the blessing of God's love enfolded us like great protective wings. When we harvested the bounty of the garden, we rejoiced in these gifts of the Great Spirit. When we awakened in the morning we could look at one another and exult just in being alive and together. This delight was a particular blessing granted by our heavenly Father, and we knew it—each and every one.

If dad was the captain and I the first lieutenant, then logically God was the general of all the armies, and we sought to so conduct ourselves.

To say that I helped to produce "quality" is, certainly, to use my own assessment of what "quality" consists of in the end product. I have no modesty about my children, for I go down the list and purr with pride in the manifestations of the particular qualities I most admire.

To meet with deep personal loss and stand up under the shock, moving on to rebuild with courage and intestinal fortitude—this I regard as the infinite measure of quality.

To have a talent and through hard work increase it a thousandfold, then still reach for a higher potential—this spells Quality with a captial Q, for it implies continual growth.

To give love packed down and running over in spite of rejection, through all vicissitudes, and with a constant faith in our Lord—this is not just quality but victory.

To have a pliant strength so that they could move into and adapt to a completely new way of life—this quality we prayed for in our children.

To be able to make a mistake in judgment and accept with patient forbearance and personal responsibility the stripes meted out by life—this rated a medal from mother.

To live with constancy, with positive action, with joy in each blessing, and with an acceptance of what we could not change—how about that for quality?

To serve God with a blazing witness and to be deemed worthy of trust in service to our country was "quality" of the highest order.

Twenty-two years ago—I cannot believe these words as I write them—we had had a very good Christmas season. The orders had poured into the little shop and both Grey Owl and I were very tired when it was over. We had worked hard, but as our hands flew there was time for talk. That is, he talked and I listened.

He spoke of the path our children should walk, that they should stay close to one another in spirit, cherish honor and integrity above all virtues, and love God beyond everything else. He talked of his people and their needs. "Most of all," he said, "we need the truth of the gospel—in its fullness." He laid the path for my research and said, "You must search the oldest records, for although we know the legends hold the key, there must be confirmation in historical record."

And one morning he told me of a dream:

"You and I," he said, "were in a great museum where all the richest treasures of the world were on display. We wandered from room to room, each one more beautiful than the last. In the grand lobby there was a stairway, and each time we passed it I wanted to go up to the next floor; for if all these wonders were down here, what must be in store up there!

"But," he continued, "each time you begged to explore one more room. So at last I couldn't wait any longer and started up the stairs without you. I saw you turn back and said, 'Well, join me when you're ready.'"

Then came the evening when, busy with getting the children ready for the night, I found him on the couch and said to myself, "How pale and tired he looks; we must rest this week."

He rose; the look in his eyes was as though he were measuring my strength, and I hesitated.

"Let's go out for coffee," he said. "Now?" I questioned.

"Now," he said.

He called the little ones and embraced them, spoke to the oldest daughter and committed them to her keeping. To David, the firstborn son of our love, he said, "You're the oldest boy, Davy; keep order in my house."

And still I did not know.

Minutes later as we sat in the coffee shop talking to friends, he turned his back on them, laughed, and collapsed in my arms.

Twenty-two years, my love, and in these earthly rooms my eyes have seen so much. I know that when I'm ready there's a stairway I will follow to find you in the upper rooms.

I thank you for the tenderness and courage with which you met both life and death. I bless you for the way you opened paths for us to follow, and your witness of the Christ we both adore. I hope he will forgive me if I say the greatest treasure that you left me is the memory of the time when we were all together—you and I and fourteen children—with love.

CHAPTER 14

Outrageous Fortune

One of the least understood areas of Indian problems is that of land claims. Many people wring their hands and grieve about the "terrible wrong done to Indian people" two hundred years ago. They are often startled to have the sympathy rejected on the grounds that the same thing is going on today.

Reporters pounce with glee on demonstrations over one claim or another but fail to give the background of the protest. Indians proclaim with sweeping statements that they sold the land and no one bothered to pay the bill. Perhaps the only way out of this labyrinth of misconception is the recipe for getting "unlost" while driving in an unfamiliar neighborhood: go back to the starting point and try again.

From the ratification of the Delaware Treaty in 1778 until after the United States Constitution was adopted in 1789, the general practice of the government was to obtain land by bargaining with the tribes rather than by force. The agreements were usually in the form of treaties. Specific areas of land were either under option to the federal government or were sold outright to that body in consideration of a price per acre, annuities, or other emoluments.

It was manifest to the Indian from an early date that the two cultures were incompatible in the same area and they, albeit reluctantly, sometimes chose to dispose of land rather than to remain in areas where they were under harassment by incoming settlers of vastly different cultural values. The depletion of game and natural foods as the influx of European settlers increased put unfamiliar economic pressures on the tribes. Piecemeal sales of land could stave off starvation for a time.

Quite early in the settlement of the eastern states, it was patent that the sales of Indian lands to individuals or to the land companies resulted in a confusion of ownership and gross exploitation. One case in point was the debacle of the controversy between the states of New York and Massachusetts and the Holland Land Company over Oneida lands in what is now New York. This controversy left no doubt that a single body must have the sole right of option.

Conflicting claims of the two states over grants of land made by the Duke of York on the one hand and Charles I on the other caused continuing bitterness between the two states. While this controversy was raging, a group of land speculators from Europe under the name "The Holland Land Company" sent representatives among the Oneidas to buy up options against the day they might be persuaded to sell.

Problems were arising within the Oneida Nation as the new settlers began to infiltrate their territory. Restrictions had been imposed very early regarding the licensing of traders. Indian people could not avail themselves of the open market but had to deal with certain specified traders. One of the first indications the

Indians had that there was not by any stretch of imagination going to be a meeting ground for the two opposing life-styles was that business transacted with the white man (as represented by the traders) had as its primary rule "friendship ceases where profits begin."

There was another very sad example of a conflict of interests which resulted in a development of factions in a nation that had heretofore prided itself on unity. Perhaps only by looking back in retrospect can we become aware of what the division of doctrines in the Christian religions must have meant to Indian people of that day.

There were various forms of worship among different Indian cultures, but within a particular culture there was a solidarity both of concept and of form. The Indian said, "We never argued about the things of God"—meaning that within his own nation certain rituals and beliefs had come down through the ages as tradition. It was not a thing to argue about or to question, and no one culture ever tried to impose its religious custom on another.

Indians were being converted to Christianity but not to an ideal of Christian brotherhood. As the various denominations moved in, they taught that the only way to be good, or to save one's soul, was to join a particular church. Thus new divisions came about between bands and often between members of a family who happened to live in areas of opposing churches.

The stage was set for the most successful gambit ever formulated: "Divide and conquer."

As factions developed among the Oneida, one or the other would sign agreements to sell, often covering the same piece of territory, thus adding fuel to the controversy between the states of New York and Massachusetts and the Holland Land Company. It was quite evident that for the protection of both buyer and seller only the federal government should have the right to purchase Indian land.

Only through viewing this background of experience in the East can we understand the foundation of later treaties with western tribes.

A study of the Oneida treaties provides an education in division by which the land base shrank from several million acres to a few hundred in the span of forty years. The first treaties with the federal government referred to the Oneida nation as a whole and covered the entire area of western New York as Oneida territory. Within a few years treaties were being signed with two groups, the Pagan Party and the Christian Party. Subsequent treaties show further division by separate treaties with four groups designated Pagan Party, Orchard Party, First Christian Party, and Second Christian Party.

The many cessions of Indian land to the United States form the basis for the alleged wrongs of fraud, duress, and unconscionable consideration for which the Indians seek redress. There are also a number of claims involving the taking of lands or Indian property without the consent of or payment to Indians.

Before 1946 the only way an Indian claim against the United States could be litigated was to obtain specific permission from Congress. The case was then given into the charge of a Court of Claims, but often the court's authority did not extend to all aspects of the tribe's claim and many important matters went unresolved.

Therefore, in 1946, Congress passed the Indian Claims Commission Act (P.L. 79-726) which created a judicial body to resolve the residue of Indian claims accruing prior to that year. It also enlarged the scope of the claims which Indians could bring against the government and specified a cutoff date of August 13, 1951, for the filing of claims.

The Court of Claims was also given continuing jurisdiction over a narrower class of claims accruing after 1946. These would include cases of alleged fraud, exploitation, mismanagement of funds or nondelivery of services.

The Commission was actually given just ten years to adjudicate all claims; but the initial 370 petitions grew to 611 complex dockets; more time and a larger staff were needed.

By 1967 the commission membership was increased from three to five and substantial staff increases were made in 1970-71. In fiscal year 1972 the commission was extended for another five-year period to April 10, 1977. After that time, any cases still pending were to be transferred to the United States Court of Claims.

A glance at the recurring extensions of the life of the commission may present a glimmer of understanding of the plaintiff's wrath at the red tape involved in the actual litigation. At least Indians have come through the harrowing experience with a detailed knowledge of the slow process of law—though for most of them it would have been cheaper to go to law school. Every day a case drags on creates a strain on an often nonexistent economy, and some of the litigation extends for many years.

In the annual report of the Indian Claims Commission, 1974, a comprehensive assessment of its work is appended. It is interesting to note, compressed into a single paragraph, the unavoidable delays and the implication of niggling details to exasperate claimants not entirely familiar with due process of law. It is to be remembered that the great majority of the tribes presenting claims have existed for several generations in the depths of poverty. For them, just to appear in court presents agonizing sacrifices—to be able to get there in the first place, and to live or commute during the months or years of litigation.

How many times has the story been told of Indians digging down in the pocket for stray dimes and quarters to finance representatives who seemed to have an idea that would speed the process? There is much to be said for the character of a people with such staying power that they are able to hang in there when it seems their case will never be resolved, and when at home the babies are hungry and there are no beans.

What are these unavoidable delays?

In the first place, to present a claim the claimants must prove that they have a case. Indian plaintiffs must show that they had a compensable property interest in the land in question. They must prove that the lands involved were held by their tribe or nation under what is known as aboriginal or "Indian title" based on continuous use or occupation of a definable area "for a long period of time." Proof of such occupancy involves detailed ethnological and historical reports. Much of the evidence is received from experts in the field of archaeology.

Other cases involve areas formerly allocated as Reservation land which for one reason or another passed from Indian occupancy. These last claims present complex decisions on the overall interpretation of Constitutional law and are among the most difficult to resolve. They present problems of titles held by white owners who may (or may not) have been innocent of any evil intent. All aspects of the claims must be carefully researched before suit is filed.

Once a suit is under way, the commission receives evidence of the fair market value of the land at the date of its acquisition by the United States. This generally is presented in reports of land appraisers and other experts hired by the plaintiffs. Then the amount of consideration in cash, goods and services, etc. which have already been paid must be adjudged.

Then there is the confusion of the Indian claimant faced with the burning question, "Whom can we trust?" The federal government whose obligation it is to promote the general interest of the majority of the people? The mercy of the courts? But what assurance is there that they are concerned with mercy? Have they shown mercy in the past? Can even Indians' attorneys be trusted? (There is money and power on the other side.) The state in which the claim is located? Perish the thought! The states have no constitutional responsibility to defend Indian land, a charge defined as Trust Responsibility of the Federal Government. In the second place, the state has sometimes been the culprit that confiscated the land to begin with.

Dizzying, isn't it?

This, of course, is only the beginning. After liability has been established and the amount thereof has been stated in an interlocutory award, the United States is entitled to present all gratuitous offsets which it claims are allowable against the award. Monies spent for the removal of Indians from one place to another, for agency or administrative purposes, for health, education, or highways are not deductible, since these considerations were covered in the original treaties.

Even in the most clear-cut cases, the due process of law is so complex that every claim settled is a major victory. Granting the infuriating delays, the mountains of red tape, the commission has succeeded in resolving the greater part of the claims presented since its inception. This does not add to the happiness of the plaintiffs who are still waiting; it is the truth, nevertheless.

A brief résumé of the situation as of 1974—to pick a year—is in order. During that year the commission entered ninety-six decisions affecting twenty-five dockets. Included in these ninety-six determinations were dismissals of eleven dockets and the entry of twenty final awards involving twenty-four dockets. The total sum awarded in fiscal year 1974 was in excess of 46 million dollars, and the total number of claims still pending was 186.

The amounts awarded run from $2,650 for one of the Seneca Nation suits to $2,286,991.54 on a combined claim of the Sisseton and Wahpeton Sioux. These are just figures in a report. Somewhere along here there are echoes of dissatisfied Indian claimants over what sounds like a lot of money. It must be remembered that these amounts represent a "settlement" which is somewhere between what the claimants want and what the defendant is willing to pay. The primary unhappiness of the claimants is something like this: any other mortgage holder would long ago have received payment in full, or he would have long since repossessed the property to resell it at a vastly increased rate per acre. Neither of these options has been available to the Indian.

Most of them, however, agree realistically that there probably isn't enough money in the world to pay for America at the present-day fair market value...so they settle for what they can get.

Once having a case resolved, the offsets calculated, and the amount of award determined, the troubles of the claimant tribes are not over. A decision must be made as to how this money will be dispensed. The tribe has the responsibility to decide whether the money will be divided on a per capita basis or invested for the good of the whole community. This is where the factions develop into wide chasms of protest from the proponents of both sides.

To an Indian family that has lived in great financial distress during years of litigation, that share looms fantastically important, though the actual amount may come a long way from providing any lasting benefits. Experience shows that tribes which have allocated the sum to community projects providing education, jobs, or facilities fare better in the long run; but it is hard to wait when one has waited so long.

A case in point is the $16 million settlement in 1975 for the Seminole's historic claim to thirty-two million acres of land comprising virtually all of Florida. Property values being what they are in the Sunshine State, not all of the Seminole are entirely satisfied with this amount. Some favor lawsuits against the state of Florida to win damages for the disruption of their lands by drainage projects and for infringements on the tribe's hunting rights.

The major dispute, however, centers around the projected allocation of money. The young leaders, most of them in their twenties and thirties, are trying to lead their people to a new affirmation of pride in their heritage, and at the same time toward increased education and job skills which they believe are necessary to survive.

Says Mike Tiger, the tribe's human resources director, "I would like to see it all invested, maybe in a bank at a good rate of interest...or in a business. It could help to solve a lot of our problems."

The problems are there: the 30 percent unemployment rate, the $2,400 average annual income, the 60 percent illiteracy, and the 67 percent school dropout rate. The same figures influence those who press for a per capita payment, although after legal fees are deducted and a substantial sum distributed to the possible 12,000 Seminole in Oklahoma, each share may be less than $2,500.

Two areas of concern provide a troubling atmosphere for Indian would-be claimants and white citizens as well. For a long time, the question of termination of federal services has been a bone of contention. Whole political careers have risen and fallen on the sharp edge of this Damocles' Sword that dangles over Indian heads. The proponents commonly hold that the settlement of a claim should result in an automatic termination of federal responsibility. Indians protest that the payment of the cash involved should not absolve the original contractors from the other obligations stated in the contract. In the instances where termination has occurred with the consequent loss of services, the reservations have been left destitute of these benefits, for the states have been unable to assume the burden, and the amount awarded the tribe has been insufficient to set up its own long-term program. Now, supposedly, this idea has proven an unhappy solution, but the specter is still there.

The other area of concern lies in the cases where land has been removed from Indian ownership without the action of Congress. The Federal Trade and Intercourse Act of 1790 states that no land of any tribe could be acquired without the consent of Congress. In a number of cases, there is evidence that parts of reservation land were preempted at some point by a state or township either through leases, parks allocated, or other means, and eventually passed into private title.

Those tribes that have instituted claims to settlement for such lands have very good prospects—if civil liberties are taken seriously. The Federal Trade Act includes other controls aside from those pertaining to Indian land. To scrap the whole act would cause great confusion in other departments; to single out for abrogation only the clause pertaining to Indian land would constitute gross discrimination. Ways have been found to get around this embarrassing dilemma, of course, but it leaves some agonizing problems about both the present and former owners. If the non-Indian owners have already paid for their lands, who's going to pay the Indians? If the land reverts to reservation status, what happens to the non-Indian owners who no longer have the right to live there? The questions can be resolved, but they involve the bitterness of Indian people who were the losers in the first place, and the anger of non-Indian owners who now find themselves in the position of the original possessors. Both sides seem to be in the same boat, and it is to be hoped they will use their paddles more gently than was done in the past. We ought to learn *something* as we go along.

One interesting little anecdote has emerged in the last few years to demonstrate that Indians at least are learning something from the experiences of the past. One young chief has been constantly besieged to lend his support to offers from the government for a certain piece of land held by this tribe. It so happens that the land in question is the most fertile part of his reservation and is presently under well-managed production. The ante has been raised repeatedly so that the total sum offered has reached what might seem very tempting proportions. His final answer is that no amount of money will be accepted by his tribe.

"Money is a perishable commodity," he says, "but we will make a trade. You give us an equal amount of land, equally as fertile, and adjoining our present holdings, and we'll talk business."

The trouble is that the only such land around there is owned by established white farmers.
Impasse.

CHAPTER 15

A Land Shadowing with Wings

My topsy-turvy world has kept me bouncing from one extreme to another, and I have no complaints about this yo-yo existence. As Grey Owl and I did when we entered on our adventure, I walk with my heart on tiptoe, marveling at the infinite variety of this exciting world. To walk the stately halls of Washington and then come home to pull weeds in a garden and know again the eternal verity of the warm earth—what have I done to deserve this?

On one whirlwind trip through Ontario I had lunch in an absolutely beautiful and gracious home...and that same evening feasted on roast venison and traditional corn bread with the Tuscaroras in New York. Incredible!

I talk with school children about Indian culture, and then try to explain modern society to Indians—which is much more difficult, believe me. But the most fulfilling times of all are when I visit friends in informal groups or congregations and we discuss our mutual faith. Many of the ideas and convictions are those I first heard from Grey Owl long before I knew what they were all about.

Not only in the church but on the streets, in business offices, on a bus, there is uneasy agreement that "something is happening here" and "it's later than we think." We cannot watch the news or read a paper without concluding that we are, indeed, in the latter days. Some of the signs are disturbing, and we have the eerie suspicion that things may get worse before they get better. There have been wars and rumors of wars in every generation but never, I think, such a complete epidemic of them. People of all nations *are* running back and forth across the earth, many of them to talk of peace...but one wonders if they have their fingers crossed behind their backs.

How terrifying it would be if we did not have this faith in a time of peace and renewal for the earth! How dreary it would be if there were not also signs of a great awakening. With many people, I watched a Pope walk the streets of New York and Washington and was impressed by the thousands of young people who cheered. They were not all Catholics; many were youths hungry for some spiritual joy in a world replete with boredom and temptation.

I read the testimony of a Messianic Jew, and it opened a whole new train of thought. In my absorption with my own faith and hopes for my own people, I had lost sight of the fact that Judah also, and particularly, is Israel. There have always been, since the time of Christ, Jews who accepted him as the Messiah foretold and described in their ancient scriptures. They were persecuted along with the rest of their people, ostracized by their brothers, and unknown to the Christian community. Until very recently, they were invisible.

Their premise is that when a Jew accepts a Messiah, prophesied throughout the Old Testament, born into a Jewish home, in a Jewish land, he becomes not a "converted" but a "completed" Jew. Semantics often get in the way of our communication with people of other cultures.

To us, "converted" may mean being awakened to Christ; to them it means to be changed from what they are. The thought of being non-Jew offends and troubles Jewish people, for the God of Abraham, Isaac, and Jacob promised that he would remember his love for their fathers and recognize them before the world. How could I, as a Christian Indian, have missed that point? It was the thought that we would somehow be non-Indian that had held us so long from the Master's touch. We must come as we are with the witness of our heritage intact, so that the symphony of praise will be complete. The Jews *have* returned to Palestine; their deserts have become productive once again; and there *are* increasing numbers "completed in their faith."

Witness is in every corner, though often we must open the eyes of faith to receive it. One of the most touching experiences of the last few years was when I joined old friends at the weekly Indian Prayer Breakfast in Washington to view the latest films of the Shroud of Turin. I had heard of it many years before and had dismissed it as "a Catholic relic." Now the research was traced and the evidence verified that it was indeed a cloth from the time period of Jesus, that pollen dust in the fibers revealed it could have come only from Palestine of that era. The narrator explained that never until the present age, when the space program had fostered the need for improved cameras and other sensitive tools, had it been possible to learn so much about it. Much of that was above my head; but as the marks of the lash appeared, the deep wounds on the scalp, the wrists, the feet and the breast, every hand at that table was joined with its neighbor. And as the battered features of the face came into focus, our tears flowed—regardless of our doctrines or the background of our faith. But the most inspiring point of all was the opinion of one scientist that the stains appeared to be more similar to those which would result from a sudden surge of power—such as shadow-pictures etched on walls after an atomic blast. Thus, *if* the shroud is genuine and if we could believe it was indeed the one on which the Savior lay, it is the witness not of his death but of his resurrection.

Of course they have not proved that this was the burial cloth of our dear Lord. Of course there will continue to be conflicting research and opinions. But I thought of Thomas and his doubts, and of the Lord saying kindly and patiently, "You find it hard to believe? Come, Thomas, touch me; I will help your unbelief."

Our times are full of increasing evidence that the things we have believed in our hearts are incredibly, wonderfully true—signals sent that say, "You find it hard to believe? Touch me, and receive more truth."

I am impatient with the idea that we should huddle under the security blanket of thinking, "Just sit still and God will do it all." He'll destroy all the wicked people, clean up the atmosphere; sweep away all the accumulation of trash with which humanity has surrounded itself—and we few will inherit a bright new world. As Grey Owl and I once did, I sit at the scarred old desk and lift my eyes to the horizon framed by my window. We were like children, imagining only the joy when at last we would see the Lord coming in glory. How we would run to meet him!

Now I am not so sure. I still feel that thrill of joy that we might meet the Master face to face, but I tremble for the questions he might ask.

"What of the Fair Land that was given to be a blessing to all humankind? Have you cherished this holy earth? Is it ready for my coming?"

Suppose he should look beyond our eager welcome to the crime-filled city streets and ravaged plains, across the seas to other lands and say, "Where are the rest of my sheep?" Shall I answer, "Well, the whole thing went down the tube, Lord. But I am here—and I've been waiting for you to clean it up and make it new again."

I know that I am often a pain in the neck to people who have a strong belief that, with enough prayer, the cloud of darkness will be lifted from the world—and with no more effort. I share that faith in prayer and believe that every effort should be preceded and attended by it. I believe that our very lives should be an act of prayer and thanksgiving.

I am reminded, however, that ninety-seven Christian Indians spent the night in prayer—locked as prisoners in the church they had built in the wilderness—and were clubbed to death in the morning. By the will of God? I cannot believe that. They were not martyrs for their faith; they were slain because a regiment made a mistake. God should not have to shoulder the blame for people's misuse of their agency to choose good or evil.

How many hundreds of thousands of parents today pray tearfully for the deliverance of their children from drugs? Yet the drugs pour into our neighborhoods in ever-increasing supply.

Maybe Someone is trying to tell us something. Maybe faith without works *is* dead faith. Maybe we are praying for the wrong thing and ought to be petitioning: "Imbue me with the strength of your Spirit that I may work with you to heal the ravaged earth."

The blessed occasions that I have spent with those who share this faith usually have brought us to some point when we have remembered that in the fullness of time we will witness to the remnant of Israel, and that this remnant will return that witness in some way enhanced and imbued with a new vitality. Many people have asked me whether I know just what hidden knowledge we might have to give in return for such a precious gift as the awakening to Christ. I do not know, of couse; for none of us can know the ultimate ways in which his purposes will come to pass. I sense a few ways in which our faith may be reaffirmed and revitalized, for I have experienced them in my own life.

For one thing, and I believe those who minister to other cultures in the world could testify of this, the very act of witnessing to people with a different language and culture enlarges our understanding of the preciousness of all the children of the earth. We learn to accept their differences and to delight in the infinite variety in which they were created. At the same time our understanding is increased, so is our humility in acknowledging that they are as important to and as beloved by the Creator as are we.

Then we begin to fully recognize the universality of God, who spoke to his children in many languages, giving them a truth to live by, each in his own particular habitat.

Finally, the witness of the "other sheep" of this part of the pasture may be the conclusive evidence of the divinity of Christ. If he was here, and in the period when he visited in human form on the earth, then he was more than mortal man. Oh, there will continue to be expeditions which attempt to prove that he could have made the voyage across the sea by fishing boat, but they will fail, for they leave out one element — time.

We cannot, and we should not, put words into the testimony of these hoped-for witnesses, for the questions will arise, "Do they truly know? Or are they simply repeating the views of the defense?" The witness must come about in the natural course. If they are able to look within their heritage and find the seeds of the Master's teachings untouched by the change and trauma of the years between, we shall all be brought closer to the time when "every knee shall bend."

In the meantime, and in the process, I believe that we are being brought face to face with the necessity to use our agency to serve either evil or good. We cannot teach love and condone hatred. We cannot reach for a Zionic society and ignore the powers of darkness that will use every means for destroying the possibility.

What of our stewardship of this blessed land—the land shadowing with wings, the land southward and the land north? Do those words have meaning for us? Let us not delude ourselves. The establishing of one small corner where a community of peace and love might safely worship and wait for his coming will be impossible unless we can establish also an outer perimeter. Do we have faith that God, himself, will be our shield? We must remember that he sends his rain on the just and the unjust. He is, indeed, our sword and shield in things of the spirit. He is concerned with the spirit; we are concerned with a material habitat where those spirits can prove themselves worthy of his kingdom. History has shown that while there have been billions who have died in their faith and gone as martyrs into the world beyond, people are vulnerable to other people. We need not speculate too much on what would happen if a world gone mad with famine and evil were to find one place where the inhabitants lived in peace and plenty.

I destroy a dream? Ah, no. The dream is true and worthy. The task of persons of faith is to enlarge the scope so that the dream can be.

The danger today is not so much in war-mongers as in carelessness of speech that inflames the passions of the world. The danger is a developing elite which threatens to destroy the human rights that we have worked to bring about for all people on the earth. The danger is from the power-seekers who, after secret combinations for so many years, now wear an open face.

This is one point of witness that will "return" from this remnant of the land shadowing with wings. Some fifteen hundred years after the destruction, they *are* the witness of the result when passion and terror consume a nation. Those fifteen centuries have not been pleasant. Survival was the prime necessity. They were harried and driven first by one another and then by throngs that swept across the land like swarms of locusts. For over two centuries they were not only forbidden to speak their language or to paint their memory-scriptures on the walls but to practice their religion. There was, indeed, in this century one last effort to destroy their faith by the confiscation of eagle feathers, their affirmation that the human spirit can fly beyond the world of pain.

It is an awesome thing to envision the witness of a people who, in spite of having had no written scripture to reinforce their religious concept, have kept its spiritual vision bright and clear.

Yes, these descendants of the Ancients have a testimony for these latter days, and it is one that will preclude any limitation of the scope of time and space. Their dreams are of vast, clean, open spaces refreshed by sun and wind. Every mile of the length and breadth of the Land Shadowing with Wings is "holy ground" to them. They will say, "Open the doors of the spirit and dare to plant the stakes of your lodge on wider ground."

Destroy the dream? Ah, no...but let the light be

strong enough to make of this whole land a beacon of hope and faith in this time of final choice.

CHAPTER 16

—and Rainbows

Leaving out the proverbial pot of gold, which no one seems to have found as yet, the best thing that can be said for rainbows is that they are symbols of hope. That ancient promise made when the Great Spirit set his bow in the heavens reminds us that Someone up there still cares.

There are several rainbows in these troubled days, signs of the sun breaking through the clouds of misery and distrust. For Indians sitting on the Reservation—jobless, frustrated, and sick to death of committees and delay they may be hard to see. And they may seem equally hidden for Urban Indians who are entrapped in poverty but ineligible for even the meager help they would have received if they had stayed at home. But they are there, these rainbows, and though we have learned by experience that the promises of humans are subject to change without notice, we have never doubted the promises of God.

Interestingly, prophecies often come to fulfillment as though in the natural course of events. I wonder, too, how many times we are unaware that we are really doing the Lord's work when we are under the impression that we are acting on our own initiative.

I seriously doubt, for instance, that legislators would stand up in meeting to say, "The good Lord is getting ready to move for these people, so let's get the show on the road." Not that they wouldn't—most of them—be happy to do some little chore along those lines (even if they knew what they were doing). I'm really not cynical about legislators, who are often good people, but their situation is an unenviable one filled with pressures. They are constantly at the mercy of lobbyists; their days are filled with meetings of the various committees, so it is no wonder they miss out on the discussions of the merits of certain pieces of legislation. They are sometimes reduced to dashing into the House to cast a last moment ballot merely on the recommendation of the loudest voice. We really ought to cheer and pass out laurels when good sound legislation is passed.

A rainbow has to start somewhere, and it is rather difficult to say at what point this particular one began. We could be very pragmatic about the whole thing and say, "It's all a natural sequence of cause and effect." But that is simply scamping the subject; the law of cause and effect is one of the Creator's natural laws by which his world is governed.

We can say, for instance, that Indians were so filled with bitterness and anger that their protest came boiling over the top and set in motion certain trends. However, Indians were boiling with bitterness through other generations, too, and nothing seemed to change. First one thing had to happen, then another, and another until at last it all began to gel.

A great many Americans have been interested in Indians; however, a great many Americans also have had serious problems of their own. Factual information on the tragic circumstances among Indian people has always been available, if one knew where to look or had any hint of the circumstances, which most Americans did not.

The media, (primarily newspapers, TV, and the motion picture industry) have not particularly distinguished themselves as purveyors of the whole truth and nothing but the truth. We get a little tired of the noble, slim, trim savage dripping feathers to his heels, standing in the glow of a campfire to receive the delegate from the White Father. Any Indian today knows that if he's lucky enough to have those eagle feathers he'd jolly well want to be very careful where he wore them...and be very sure he had the White Father's permission to have them at all.

Just once we'd like to see a pot-bellied Indian, obese from his diet of starch, fending off yet another committee that has come to see if he needs a job, and if so, why.

In common with many Indians, I had had scant patience with the militant groups—not for lack of sympathy with the cause, for during the period of violent protest I was sick at heart and insulted as an American with the record of abuse I had found in my research. My impatience was with the method employed. I could not see how we could win friends and influence people by breaking their windows. Nor could I see that the dedicated leaders could accomplish much while incapacitated by bullet wounds or buried in some jail.

I had to actually hear those famous words, "Brave up, brother, it's a good day to die," to feel that tender rush of love for these unhappy sons and daughters of my people. They actually were willing to sacrifice their lives and freedom, and many of them never recovered from that agonizing crusade. I hope we may find that among the other storm clouds theirs was one that brought the rainbow. For we do have a rainbow; whether there is treasure at the end of it remains to be seen.

On January 2, 1975, in a joint resolution of both houses of Congress, Public Law 93-580 was passed. By this piece of legislation, the American Indian Policy Review Commission was established. It provided for the most comprehensive review of Indian policy, both past and present; and through its findings suggestions would be offered to the Congress for legislation that would affect all relationships between tribal and federal/state governments in the future. It was to be, in fact, a committee to end committees.

Congress declares that it is timely and essential to conduct a comprehensive review of the historical and legal developments underlying the Indians' unique relationship with the federal government in order to determine the nature and scope of necessary revisions in the formulation of policies and programs for the benefit of Indians.

The commission was composed of three members of the Senate appointed by the president pro tempore of the Senate, and three members from the House of Representatives appointed by the speaker. They were to select five members of the commission from the Indian community, and they had available to them a wide choice of fully qualified and deeply committed Indian leaders. Of these five, three were to be selected from Indian tribes recognized by the federal government, one to represent Urban Indians, and one from a tribe not on federal status.

It is to be noted that this was of historical importance because it was the first time since the United States came into being that a commission was established with major Indian representation reporting directly to the Congress. The serious intent of the Congress was evidenced also in the selection of Congressional members who had been actively involved with Interior and Indian Affairs.

Whether one is trying to become better acquainted with Indians as spiritual brothers and sisters or as fellow citizens, a brief sketch of the members of the Commission will reveal two major and important facts. One is the variety and complexity of issues facing Indian people today; the other is the high degree of professionalism and expertise developed among Indian leaders.

From the United States Senate:

Honorable James Abourezk, Chairman, (Democrat, South Dakota). Born and reared on the Rosebud Sioux Reservation; chairman of the Senate Subcommittee on Indian Affairs, chairman of the Senate Subcommittee on Separation of Powers, and a member of the Select Committee on Small Business. (He had fostered the passage of several important Indian Bills, including the present P.L. 93-580.)

Honorable Lee Metcalf. (Democrat, Montana) Member of the Senate Subcommittee on Indian Affairs; chairman of the Senate's Subcommittee on Minerals, Materials, and Fuels; chairman of the Senate's Subcommittee on Reports, Accounting and Management. (He had been instrumental in the passage of favorable Indian legislation, including the Comprehensive Indian Act of 1972.)

Honorable Mark Hatfield. (Republican, Oregon) Ranking Minority Member on both the Energy Research and the Water Resources Subcommittees; a member-at-large of the Senate Select Committee on Nutrition and Human Needs. (He was instrumental in the passage of the Umatilla Judgment Fund legislation and the Klamath Forest Bills; also cosponsored Senator Jackson's Indian Health Bill.)

From the United States House of Representatives:

Honorable Lloyd Meeds. Vice-chairman (Democrat, Washington) Chairman of the House Indian Affairs Subcommittee; member of the Subcommittee on National Parks and Recreation, Territorial and Insular Affairs; and the Subcommittee on Water and Power Resources. (He backed the Alaskan Native Claims Act, Indian Education Act of 1972, and the Menominee Restoration Bill, for which he received the National Congress of American Indians' Congressional Award.)

Honorable Sidney R. Yates. (Democrat, Illinois) Served in the House of Representatives since 1948 except for a two-year period during which he was a United States Representative to the Trustee Council of the United Nations; chairman of the Interior Subcommittee of the House Appropriations Committee; a member of the Transportation and Legislative Subcommittees.

Honorable Sam Steiger. (Republican, Arizona) A member of the Interior and Insular Affairs Committees; served as a ranking member of the Subcommittee on Government Labor, Subcommittee on Individual Rights, and the Subcommittee on Public Lands.

The Indian members of the commission had distinguished themselves in past service to their people, and they represented a cross section of Indians from coast to coast.

Commissioner Ada Deer. One of the most outstanding women of the century; left law school to defend her tribe against termination, and is credited with being the most important single force behind the success of the Menominee Restoration Act.

Commissioner Jake Whitecrow. A former Quapaw Tribal Chairman who is Quapaw and Seneca-Cayuga Indian; served on his Tribal Business Committee since 1953, and was director of the Intertribal Council of Northeastern Oklahoma, which is a representative of the Eastern Shawnee, Seneca-Cayuga, Wyandot Quapaw, Ottawa, Peoria, Miami, and Modoc tribes.

Commissioner John Borbridge. Head of Sealaska Corporation, which is one of the twelve Native Alaskan Corporations established under the Native Alaskan Claims Act, for which he lobbied extensively. Past-president of the Tlingit-Haida Central Affairs Commission of Alaska and also a member of the Financial Advisory Board of the American Indian National Bank.

These were the members from Federally Recognized Tribes. Representing Urban Indians:

Commissioner Louis R. Bruce, Mohawk and Oglala Sioux; former Commissioner of the United States Bureau of Indian Affairs (1969-1972); active in the formation of the National Tribal Chairman's Association, and the American Indian National Bank. (After leaving the Bureau of Indian Affairs, he served as a Senior Fellow of the Antioch Law School and assisted in the establishment of the Coalition of Eastern Native Americans, in which he served as Finance Director.)

Representing the Nonfederally Recognized Tribes:

Commissioner Adolph Dial, a Lumbee Indian; chairman of the American Indian Studies Department of Pembroke State University, and a member of the American Indian Advisory Council for the United States Department of Health, Education and Welfare's Office of Civil Rights. (He was also a member of the Board of Trustees of the American Indian Historical Society.)

The implementation of the work was carried on by

eleven task forces composed of three members each, a majority of whom were of Indian descent. The scope of the investigation proposed was monumental, and to carry out its work the commission had access to every record or document, the power to subpoena witnesses and to administer oaths for testimony. The areas to be covered would include, *but not be limited to,* the following:

1. A study and analysis of the Constitution, treaties, statutes, executive orders and judicial interpretations to determine the attributes of the unique relationship between the federal government and Indian tribes and their land or resources

2. A review of the policies, practices, and structure of the federal agencies charged with protecting Indian resources or providing services, with a management study of the Bureau of Indian Affairs

3. An examination of the statutes and procedures for granting federal recognition and extending services to Indian communities and individuals

4. The collection and compilation of data regarding the extent of Indian needs past and present

5. An exploration of the feasibility of alternative bodies which could fully represent Indians at the national level of government to provide Indians with maximum participation in policy formation and program development (Sound of bugles, please!)

6. A consideration of alternative methods to strengthen tribal government so the tribes might fully represent their members and, at the same time, guarantee the rights of individual Indians

7. The recommendation of such modification of existing laws, procedures, and practices as would, in the judgment of the commission, best serve to carry out the declaration of purposes for which it was formed.

The scope of research carried on by those dedicated men and women was awesome. They had one year in which to read, assess, summarize and report on every treaty, every piece of legislation, every complaint, and every court decision occurring since the first settler came to America.

In six months following the completion of the report, the commission would evaluate the results and prepare recommendations to Congress on the proposed legislation that would resolve the disaster known as Indian Affairs.

Nor were commission members content simply to sit in the office and read; they also went into the field to sit in on tribal councils and to encourage individual Indians of the smallest, most forgotten areas to voice their hopes and complaints. Their task was often agonizing. To digest in one year the ugly record of neglect or of deliberate genocidal programs must have required, first of all, a strong stomach. Indians at the grass roots level are not always impressed with academic degrees or titles, for these do not always spell loyalty to the folks at home. The task force members were at times subjected to the professional advice and warning of more experienced political leaders: "Be careful! Don't ask for too much, Remember, with one stroke of the pen, Congress could wipe your people out of existence."

What was amazing about the members of this remarkable group was that they were not only armed to the teeth with experience and expertise but deeply committed to their people. They were bound and determined that this would not be "just one more committee," that from the largest to the smallest tribe, there would be a new day for Indian people.

They plowed into tons of fact and figures and it was worse, much worse, than any of them could have imagined. Even those Indians coming out of a background of intimate knowledge of the suffering of their own people were sickened as the evidence accumulated. Every agency of the government involved with Indian Affairs revealed mismanagement or misappropriation of funds, nondelivery of services, or blatant disregard of duty. The Bureau of Indian Affairs was *not* the worst of the lot, but it was the whipping boy for the sins of all the others.

These were not nebulous areas of a breakdown in communication through a bureaucratic system, nor were they matters of ancient history. These were human problems of this day and time, and they involved the agony of childless parents and tearful children.

Every Indian has either known the loss of family and identity with a community, or knows a friend who has suffered this loss. A very common complaint against churches, or against social workers, has been: "They take our children." We did not know just how general was the practice until the figures began to emerge. These statistics involved research of the period 1969-1975.

1. 1974-75: A minimum of 24 percent of *all* Indian children were either in foster homes, adoptive homes, and/or boarding schools against the best interests of families, tribes, or communities.

2. Surveys of states with large Indian populations showed that approximately 25 to 35 percent of the children were separated permanently from their communities.

I read these figures and my heart breaks. Tens of thousands of children since it began—*our* children—would never know the precious sense of belonging with their people. Tens of thousands of parents would look to the horizon and wonder, "Where is my child this day?"

What can people be thinking of, I wondered. Don't

they know we love our children? "If you cut us, do we not bleed?" I remembered the people I met along the way, pressing forward a dark-eyed two- or three-year old. "Isn't he wonderful? We got him in Arizona." Or Wisconsin. Or New Mexico. And at my look of shock: "Oh, it's all right. His parents didn't want him. The social worker arranged everything quite legally."

I'm sure.

The methods were varied, but they became plain in the research. To remove a child, legally, from its parents, there has to be proof of neglect or abuse. In the case of Indians physical abuse can be ruled out as a cause—far less than 1 percent of the cases showed any evidence of this unnatural evil. Here are the most common methods.

1. Many social workers are ignorant of Indian cultural values and social norms. Far less do they understand the dynamics of the extended family. A child may have scores of relatives who are counted as equally responsible with his parents. Social workers often consider leaving a child with someone outside the nuclear family as neglect; they make inappropriate decisions and discover neglect where none exists.

2. Poverty, poor housing, lack of modern plumbing, and overcrowding may be cited as neglect.

3. The parents either are not informed about or are pressured into agreement. In times of family crisis such as ill health or loss of income, Indian parents are persuaded to sign waivers granting temporary custody to the state; these are used for the permanent removal.

4. In simple abductions, parents are tricked into signing what they believe to be permission for a child to visit an off-reservation missionary or interested tourist, then find it was a waiver for adoption.

This issue touched me so deeply that it was almost with a sense of guilt that I looked back across the happy years with my own children. Every struggle, every obstacle faded into nothing beside the thankfulness that they and I had been together. I was also inclined to tack it on at the end of every other issue.

"Strengthen tribal government." Of course! This is as logical as striving for better civic government in any community. We need good tribal courts and local law enforcement so we will have jurisdiction over the placement of our children. Surely this is not too much to ask!

I was impelled to Washington, D.C. As often as possible, having no real task there, I sat in fascinated wonder through the sessions when the task forces made their periodic reports to the commissioners. My heart sang and I heard the old drums. As the talk turned to the sovereignty of tribal governments the Senators began to draw back, cautioning that "the American people would not like that word." Keeping silent, as well I should, I shouted in my mind, *"Tell* them! It means having a voice in our own community! It means no more children snatched away. It means control of our own property, of courts that see us as human beings, not as 'bad Indians.' "

I wanted to run up and down the Beloved Land crying for joy to all the people. "Hang in there! This time it really *is* going to be all right. This time they mean what they say!'

During one of those visits to Washington I was a guest at the Indian Prayer Breakfast which was well attended by the commission members when they were not off on their missions in the field. As I rose to speak to them, it came to me once more that here I stood, with no academic credits at all, nothing but my love for my people. But they were not thinking of my deficiencies. I was one more Indian, and they were listening with their hearts. At the close of my talk, one woman rose to voice the thought that all of us seem caught up in some mighty force which, after all the generations of despair, would at last provide a climate in which we could be redeemed as human beings.

It was, at that time, too early to predict just what would be the outcome of this historic commission. A few indications were emerging, though they were several months away from final recommendations. One thing was becoming apparent; no single piece of legislation would solve the myriad problems of Indians in all parts of the country. Any legislation would probably be on a general policy level. Better representation of Indians at a federal level would surely result.

One very possible result—and one long needed—might be the formation of an Independent Agency for Indian Affairs outside the Department of Interior. The present system has been stultifying to Indian people, unwieldy of management, expensive in the allocation of time and funding. When we consider that the primary function of the Department of Interior is to manage the natural resources for the American people, it is not surprising that the Bureau of Indian Affairs emerges as simply the lowest drawer, or that it often constitutes a conflict of interests embarrassing to the department itself.

Legislation to clarify the status of tribes as "Nations within a Nation" is essential, and the American public is entitled to have defined just what is meant by the word "sovereignty." No community in the United States would tolerate for one moment having little or no voice in the management of local affairs, of inadequate staffing or choice in the matter of law enforcement, of having no voice in the administration of education or control over the rearing of children, no choice in the matter of health care. This is what sovereignty is all about—to have control over one's own life and property. It has nothing to do with conquest or with the fragmentation of a united nation.

Recognition of *all* Indian people on or off the reservation as being entitled to their heritage by birth and the recognition of their tribe, and their right to such services as are generally to be available to the Indian community was a priority high on the list.

One thing was certain; we had now reached that part of the ceremony when we were required to "speak now or forever hold our peace." Indians who had suffered in silence or stormed city hall in protest now had the golden opportunity to speak out at a level where it might do some good. Americans who claimed to "love Indians" now had a chance to require Congress to enact legislation that would forever get rid of this embarrassing stain on the nation's conscience.

Toward the last few months of the research, the staff began to change as professional writers and political experts moved in to assist in the compilation of the massive reports. One began to hear comments such as, "Well, now that the folk heroes are going home, we can get on with the job."

If these were "folk heroes" let us have more of them! I salute you, folk heroes, and I will never forget you. When the drums beat, calling the people to the veteran's dance, I shall dance in your honor.

Well, we shall see.

Regardless of the outcome of the commission, this is the time of the testing of our convictions. Indians who hold dear their status as nations will have to return to the old wisdom that to be of the people is to hold ourselves responsible for contributing to their well-being. There will always be powerful enemies who believe that the treaties should be abrogated. There will always be the "tourist types" who believe that if we are allowed to have a pow-wow once in a while we should be content. Now we are required to stand in dignity and self-respect, to prove once and for all that a nation can exist without conquest, save over sin and unrighteousness.

The American people will be called on to search within their consciences to see whether freedom for all means the freedom to be different from the dominant society, or if it means only "so long as you are just like me."

This, at last, is the time when all of us must "put our money where our mouths are." This, at last, after the generations of storm and dreary weather, is the day of the rainbow.

95TH CONGRESS
1ST SESSION

H.R. 9054

IN THE HOUSE OF REPRESENTATIVES

SEPTEMBER 12, 1977

MR. CUNNINGHAM introduced the following bill; which was referred to the Committee on Interior and Insular Affairs

A BILL

To direct the President to abrogate all treaties entered into by the United States with Indian tribes in order to accomplish the purposes of recognizing that in the United States no individual or group possesses subordinate or special rights, providing full citizenship and equality under law to Native Americans, protecting an equal opportunity of all citizens to fish and hunt in the United States, and terminating Federal supervision over the property and members of Indian tribes, and for other purposes.

Be it enacted by the Senate and House of Representatives of the United States of America in Congress assembled, That this Act may be cited as the "Native Americans Equal Opportunity Act".

SEC. 2. (a) The President of the United States shall, as soon as practicable after the date of enactment of this Act,

I

abrogate all treaties entered into between the United States and any Indian tribe.

(b) The President, in carrying out the provisions of this act, shall—

(1) provide that any real property which is held in trust by the United States on behalf of an Indian tribe and to which such Indian tribe is entitled, on the date of enactment of this act, to exclusive use and occupancy shall be (A) alloted, in fee simple and in severalty to the individual adult members of the tribe (as determined by an enrollment) with priority being given to those individuals with the greatest amount of Indian blood; or (B) conveyed, if a majority of the adult members of the tribe so indicate in an election, in fee simple to a tribal corporation for the purpose of enabling such corporation to hold such property in trust for the tribe;

(2) provide that all property allotted or conveyed under paragraph (1) (and all persons residing thereon and all acts committed thereon) shall be subject to the laws of Federal, State, and local governments;

(3) provide that any funds deposited to the credit of the tribe in the United States Treasury shall be (A) allotted to the individual adult members of the tribe; or (B) transferred, if a majority of the adult

II

members of the tribe so indicate in an election, to the tribal corporation described in paragraph (1) for the purpose of enabling such corporation to hold such funds in trust for the tribe;

(4) provide that hunting and fishing rights derived

by the Indian tribe from a treaty shall be abrogated, and the members of such tribe shall be subject to Federal, State, and local laws governing hunting and fishing; and

(5) provide that there be no taking without just compensation of any property right specifically created for a particular individual by any such treaty.

(c) After the completion of the abrogation of the treaties with an Indian tribe under this Act, the President shall publish in the Federal Register an appropriate proclamation of such completion. Thereafter individual members of the tribe shall not be entitled to any of the services performed by the United States for Indians because of their status as Indians, all statutes of the United States which affect Indians because of their status as Indians shall no longer be applicable to the members of the tribe, and the laws of the several States shall apply to the tribe and its members in the same manner as they apply to other citizens or persons within their jurisdiction.

(d) In the case of any Indian tribe with respect to

III

which treaties have been abrogated prior to the date of enactment of this Act or with respect to which no treaties were entered into but which remain under the supervision of the Federal Government, the President shall, as soon as practicable after the date of enactment of this Act, take steps to assure that such supervision is terminated, the completion of such termination is published in the Federal Register, and the provisions of subsection (c) apply to the members of such tribe.

(e) the President shall issue whatever regulations are necessary to carry out the provisions of this Act.

(f) For purposes of this Act, the term "Indian tribe" means any Indian tribe, band, nation, or other organization group or community, including any Alaskan Native village or regional or village corporation as defined in or established pursuant to the Alaskan Native Claims Settlement Act.

CHAPTER 17

So Now You Know

Like a cold fish across the face, isn't it, after our sunny words of the last chapter?

This, the first piece of legislation proposed after the agonizing year of research, before the recommendations of the American Indian Policy Review Commission had had time to solidify, will, I am sure, come as a rude shock to non-Indian readers. Indians will not be surprised—having had two hundred years of experience in hopes aroused and dashed aborning.

Nevertheless, let us consider this *soit dit* Equal Opportunity for Indians and its possible impact on people who are probably going to reassure themselves by saying, "It could never happen to us. We're Americans." At the risk of being redundant, let me settle that first.

Under existing law Indians are recognized as full citizens and are charged with equal responsibility for all taxes except those pertaining to reservation and/or lands held in trust by the federal government. It is true that the tribes also occupy a special status in relation to the United States. It is perhaps to their credit that Indians, having had citizenship conferred on them without actively seeking it, stack up very well in their duties as citizens with Americans in general. With the exception of the tax-exempt land, they fulfill all the obligations of other citizens.

There has been a recurring argument over whether Indians are liable for conscription into the armed forces. This has never been fully tested and, in fact, would be difficult to test, since their ratio of voluntary enlistments has been disproportionately high in every war involving their country. Approached on the question of support of the draft in World War II, some of the chiefs offered not just the eighteen- to twenty-six-year-old youths but every man between the ages of sixteen and sixty.

One juicy little tidbit which came to light during the commission report was that Indian money had played an important part in the financing of the War of 1812. What Indian money? Why, initial payments for land vacated by Indians, held in trust until such nebulous time as they "could handle their own affairs." This was perfectly legal and aboveboard...actually, most commendable that a trustee should invest his clients' funds in a good, solid venture (and what could be more solid than the future of America?).

Personally, I am not much concerned with who suggested it or how much money was involved. I am inclined to believe that Indians of that era would have been entirely compliant in such an allocation of their funds. I think they were experiencing enough difficulty adjusting to one change in population and resolved that it was not going to happen again.

The name of this proposed bill is a gross misrepresentation. A cursory examination reveals that there is not one section which gives Native Americans any right other than what they have had in the past; on the contrary, it is designed to strip away such rights as they have had.

In section 2, the treaties in question are actually bills of sale for specified pieces of land in consideration of a price per acre and/or certain obligations on the part of the purchaser. Indians do not have universal rights of hunting and fishing except for specific designations of territories in the individual treaties. The major treaties in question usually include the obligation on the part of the federal government to provide education, health care, assistance in establishing an economic base, and a trust responsibility over Indian money and resources. Though many mistakes have been made in the past in the administration of education, and though health care service has been tragically inadequate, no one involved in Indian Affairs—including Indians—would doubt for one minute that without federal supervision of the programs and resources, Indians would have been subject to gross exploitation by private power interests.

Indian people are not inferior intellectually, nor are they lacking in perception. The quiet circumstances of reservation life do, however, produce a special vulnerability to more professional operators. In the past, where federal services have been terminated, it has been the experience that within a few years land holdings have dissipated, health conditions have deteriorated, and the states have been unable to assume the extra burden of education, health, and welfare.

It is to be remembered that not all Indians are at present on federal status. Among those not under such administration, the Indian communities are the most socially and economically deprived in the nation.

Section 2 (b). This is an attempt to repeat the Allotment Act which has resulted in three generations of chaos. As the descendants of the original allottees multiplied, there developed such a confusion of heirship that an individual may claim as little as a few feet of the original property. Present Indian holdings, in the main, are not amenable for small farming. Much of the southwestern land is arid or semidesert requiring larger acreage per head of grazing stock. The ongoing competition for water rights between the states and the Indian communities is not likely to be assuaged by breaking up tribal lands into individual tracts. Plans for land improvement and irrigation would be beyond the scope of a tribal corporation, certainly beyond possibility to individuals, and would place an intolerable burden on the states. In other words, deteriorating communities of struggling small farmers would be drying up in desert sands.

This proposition would pose only one solution for Indian families—to disperse and take their chances in a life-style and a society in which many would be poorly prepared to survive.

Indians are not "confined" to reservations; they are free to leave at any time and to stay as long as they wish. Where they continue to live in the reservation community, the reasons are very much the same as for other citizens, especially for those with a background of rural or small-town origin. Their particular skills may serve them well within their own communities but be totally unsuited to the twentieth century job market. They may prefer to live close to their families and friends—and be willing to pay the price for this privilege in slower material progress. It is to be assumed that it is part of the American way of life that individuals be free to pursue their own particular dream, to live where they choose to live without coercion and without reparations if they choose to remain in status quo.

Under subtitle B (1), section 2, there is a glaring discrepancy—the conveyance of real property to a tribal corporation. The intent of this act was apparent in its introduction: that tribes "constitute a group with subordinate or special rights" and must therefore cease to exist.

It is difficult to define exactly what a tribe is or translate just what it means to Indians, whether on the reservation or not. It is their personal identity and involvement with a specific community (I am using the word in its broader sense) having a common history, values, and customs. It is inconceivable that the tribal concept will disappear from Indian consciousness regardless of how many laws are passed. Actually, the very word Indian is a manufactured term. It may be used for convenience, or because it is required for identification, but self-image is tied to Sioux, Navajo, Hopi, or other tribal lineage.

Further, Indians most aware of their tribal relationship have fewer identity crises than any other group, regardless of age or condition.

Having recognized this incontrovertible fact, we must still be prepared for the logical next question: "Why do Indians need to have 'special rights,' special status, or even special governing bodies?"

Aha! Let us now get down to the heart of this thing. Let's begin with a hypothetical situation which ought to touch the raw nerve of every good and true American. Suppose you have a piece of land which you decide to sell but you wish to retain the mineral rights. You and the buyer agree to this condition and the price. He takes his own sweet time paying for it, but you go along with the delay for several reasons, including the fact that the development of those mineral rights will one day be practicable. Imagine your reaction if you find that not only has he been mining that stuff all those years but he now proclaims that your retention of the mineral rights constituted a "special right" to which you were not entitled. You know the anwer to that one. You would have him off the land and into the courts before the could say Jack Anderson.

Here's another one. You are in business and a situation arises in which you are finally able to make a deal with a competitor in a contract that will be to your mutual benefit. He looks into your background, however, and finds that in a similar situation you have simply torn up former contracts if it became expedient. You are likely to get a very cool reception.

The rights defined in the treaties regarding the retention of hunting or fishing privileges in certain territories are no more "special" than the right of any property owner to define his interest in the retention of mineral resources. And contracts made between individuals, corporations, or nations should be no less binding whether they involve Indians or other people.

As a matter of fact, from the standpoint of other Americans, it is difficult to see why the tribal concept should be offensive. Indian communities are very much like specific areas among the general population. Their resources, problems, and solutions may differ in some degree, but so do the problems of non-Indian communities differ one from another. I submit that it would be a healthier solution, and more in keeping with the American ideal, to strengthen tribal government of local Indian communities just as we attempt to develop strong civic government in other areas. Indians *ought* to have jurisdiction over their local school systems, over local law enforcement, and certainly the right to decide which commercial developers offer the best contracts for mining their resources. If these are "special rights," then under such proposed legislation most local non-Indian communities will be in violation of the law.

Tribalism is the life-blood of Indians. It provided a foundation of many thousands of years experience in the particular and peculiar circumstances which were the most comfortable and rewarding in the life of its people; but beyond the hopes and dreams of this minority of minorities just beginning to trust again looms the threat to our national credibility. By what wild stretch of the imagination could any criticism, vocal or implied, be leveled against any nation in the world where human rights are in question, if by a stroke of the pen we can wipe a whole people out of existence? What a farce would be the signing of treaties with other nations if those made at the foundation of our country could be so easily abrogated!

Before we consider the particular "special rights" that concerned the perpetrators of this proposed legislation, let us take a close look at the question of assimilation. It bothers many Americans that at a time when efforts are being made to integrate minority groups into the general society, Indians seem to prefer to "flock by themselves."

The word "community" has various definitions. Webster's dictionary contains the following:

1. A unified body of individuals; as,
   a. a state or commonwealth
   b. the people with common interests living in a particular area
   c. an interacting population of various kinds of individuals in a common location
   d. a group of people with a common characteristic or interest living together within a larger society
   e. a group linked by a common policy
   f. a body of persons or nations having a history of social, economic, and political interests in common

The interesting point here is that in every criterion, we could substitute the word "tribe" for "community" and be well within the bounds of the definition.

What exactly is meant by "assimilation"? That everybody must be cut to the same pattern—a nation of rubber-stamp nonpersonalities? That every last American must be fired with the ambition to rush off to the largest urban area and sink into invisibility like a drop of water in the ocean? If so, we must somehow eliminate farm communities with grange activities that parallel tribal meetings. We must exorcise the very possibility of any type of religious community which would obey a higher law.

There are Indians today in every profession... Indians living in penthouses and in the suburbs. They have no more "left their people" than the local pharmacist's son who gets himself elected to Congress. They simply have chosen a sphere of action which takes them, either temporarily or for an extended period, outside their former environment. It does not change the fact they were born into a tribal group any more than it would make them less American if they chose to stay home and herd sheep.

We should all, perhaps, ask ourselves the question, "Are *we* assimilated?" Do we determine our life-style by someone else's rule or our own choice? Do we wear the same colors, imbibe the same brew, observe holidays in the same detail, live in the same kind of housing?" Maybe we are no longer sure exactly what we do mean by "assimilation." We *think* we mean something like this: that all Americans have the right to the American ideal, the right—and the obligation—to express the dream according to their talents and inclinations... to be active in community or national affairs or to avoid them. That's the way we operate.

So do Indians. Some of them work in the cities; some stay on the reservation. Some enjoy meeting people from other walks of life; some prefer their own families and friends. What's the big deal about "assimilation"?

We may have the best intentions in the world about equal opportunity—and it is a foregone conclusion that this country should be grounded in equality under the law, but all people need not—indeed, *cannot*—have equal goals.

The danger in this kind of legislation lies in its preamble: "To accomplish the purposes of recognizing that in the United States, no individual or group possesses subordinate or special rights." *Special rights!* We all, thank God, have special rights, and we should guard them well. We know at last that the old saw about the "melting pot" was a myth. America, thankfully, is a land of many diverse communities functioning very comfortably within their own frameworks but unified in the purpose to "protect and defend" their mutual nation.

In the last analysis, perhaps this proposed Act was not intended to interfere with the special rights of anyone—except Indians. For, as we get into it, we find that the rights which most offend the authors are those which deal with Indian hunting and fishing. That's the nub of it. Remember the controversy on the West Coast over Indian Fishing Rights? Interestingly enough, this "Equal Opportunity for Indians" bill was introduced by Mr. Cunningham, the Representative from the State of Washington (which might lead us to the conclusion that he was less concerned with equal opportunity for Indians than he was with getting rid of those embarrassing treaties). Let us not be too critical of Congressman Cunningham; he is answerable to the citizens of his state and specifically to the powerful fishing industries and the sportsmen's organizations. How does he, and the special interest groups who put the pressure on him, define the difference between those groups who have the "special right" to take to themselves the entire control of fishing rights in their area and the "special right" of the Indians who claim a share under a solemn treaty made with the American people?

In view of the fact that HR 9054 is obsolete, some may wonder why I become so discombobulated about a bill that is out of date.

HR 9054 was not defeated; it was held at bay by many voices until the session closed and it was too late for a vote. Its threat will lurk in Indians' consciousness reminding them once more that in every improvement or consideration they have sought, someone was there to warn: "Be careful; don't ask for too much. You know that Congress could wipe you out of existence." Indians have lived with that threat for many generations.

What bothers me even more, I think, is the threat of what is called "legislative erosion" to our Constitution. Americans have long lived with and proclaimed their faith in that noble document. Every single incumbent in office has sworn under oath to "uphold and defend the Constitution of the United States." Through our carelessness or lack of attention, or through apathy or self-interest, generations yet unborn may find themselves apologizing for "what was done to Americans" by their own ancestors.

This act, and all the progeny it will spawn, those numberless modifications and ambiguities of phrase, may be the opening wedge of a gradual erosion of all the "special rights" that have been won so dearly.

The rights that are lost may be every American's!

CHAPTER 18

Reveille at Paint Creek

I am tired. Here beneath the fine old maples, a lawn chair has been placed and I sit idle at last. The white yarn lies softly in my lap. The crochet hook has fallen to the ground; I am too tired to bend and pick it up.

There is a breeze from the lake. It lifts my hair and brushes like soft feathers on my cheek. "Be still," it says. "Be still and wait for healing."

There is no one at home today. I am alone with the trees and the sun-dappled lawn and the breeze. I need not smile brightly today and say, "Of course, my dear; I'm quite all right."

I rise and lay the yarn aside, take up my shawl and walk the sunny path to where the woods begin. The path is long; the grasses touch the fringe and mingle there. The dimness of the forest closes me in secret from the world, and there I go to Earth. My shawl over my head, my head upon her breast, I weep. My tears are for my people and their hopes; and for the dream so long delayed. My tears are for my country, and my prayers that all its noble concepts and its honor will be true. Oh, let it not have been an idle dream.

"Oh, hold it firmly in your hands, dear Lord; there is so little time. There is so much of arrogance and greed. Forgive us, dear my Lord, the power of darkness is so strong...."

I hear soft laughter. Is it the brook? It is a Warrior rimmed with light.

"Our King is stronger still."

I lift my head and dry my tears. And I remember.

* * * * *

There was a breathless excitement as we gathered that Friday morning for the Indian Prayer Breakfast. The hurry and bustle of the Capitol Building in Washington had not yet begun; the corridors echoed with our steps.

"Do you *know* who our guest is this morning?" Whispers...a joining of hands. We could hardly breathe for excitement.

Suddenly, he was there; this small, quiet man in a flowered shirt, a faded scarf about his head. A Hopi priest with a tradition of faith ancient before the first Spaniard disembarked. Prophecies so long repeated, so jealously guarded they were at once a shield and a banner.

Quietly and without oratory, he spoke to us: the GS 13's in their business suits, the smart, professional women with braided hair and beaded earrings: the Cherokee, the Narragansett, the Lakota and the Cree...the Navajo, Zuni, and the Mohawk. Those who knew, and those who were not so sure, sat quietly waiting.

"What I want to tell you," he began, and smiled a little, "is that it is later than you think. The Hopi people have prophecies handed down from so many generations back that even we cannot count them. Each generation has learned them and taught them to the next. Sometimes they were hard to understand. It was like a riddle, but we didn't try to solve it, only keep it going."

He unrolled a strip of hide painted with crude symbols; hands reached to hold it wide.

"There were to be some signs," he said, "There would come a time when great beasts would roar across the plains, but not on hooves. Their voices would be like thunder."

Our twentieth century eyes saw trains.

"And many smaller beasts, carrying many people, riding like the wind. Then would come a time when men would talk through cobwebs in the sky."

The telephone! And radio!

"Next," he said, "there would be roads in the sky, and men would travel on them."

He paused and turned to the last symbol on the banner. It was the moon.

"This," he said, "is the last sign."

There was no need for questions.

"The Hopi people have always believed that someday a Great Elder Brother who has been gone a long time would come back; but first these things had to happen. What we were supposed to do was to wait until we saw them, and then to tell all people to get ready. Indian people have a lot to do. Thay have fallen into evil ways. They must get rid of alcohol and all bad habits they have learned in this modern world. They must strengthen their spirits, live righteous lives. They must make of their lands a place of peace and good feeling; for a time is coming when the world will be full of trouble, and many people will be troubled in spirit. When that time comes, if your spirit is strong, you can help them wait through the dark time. That is all I have to say."

He sat down and drank his coffee, just as though he had not shattered the glass windows of the world.

Later, as we sat talking about it, one after another of the brilliant, successful leaders, many of them half in tears, said, "What are we doing here?"

And many of them said, "I'm going home to my people; for that's where I want to be when it happens."

And when it came my turn to speak, I was filled with fear; for who was I to tell them what to do? But I said, "No. No, I think you will not—not yet. You are the vanguard to see that your people will *have* a place to strengthen their spirits."

And they laughed, saying, "She did it to us again." And I was very proud of them, for I knew that they would stay.

Here, in the place of healing, I remember another young man who shared a testimony with us—same place, another time.

"When I came to Washington, I was pretty militant. I didn't care about other Indians; I just wanted to get some help for my own people. Now, through the fellowship we have known together, I have learned that what I want for *my* people is what I want for all Indians; and what I want for Indians is what I want for all—the right to live in dignity and self-respect."

And after all this, full of excuses and self-pity, I had fled to nurse my feeble wounds. I am half blind, my feet hurt and my heart also. I am ashamed before my Lord.

So I rise, retrieve my worn moccasins, and prepare for another journey.

CHAPTER 19

The Eagles Are Gathering Upon the Land

I have flown with the eagles at last and though ours were fledgling wings, we felt the power of developing pinions and knew that our flight would be strong, indeed.

The American Indian Peoples' Ministries of the Reorganized Church of Jesus Christ of Latter Day Saints had been in operation for several years. With incomparable vision, the church had moved into a new concept of ministry. There were to be no fiery preachments, no threat of hell; instead, there was a willingness to listen as well as to teach. Led—no, guided—first by Seventy Pete Gibbs and later by Apostle Bill Higdon, we were to search the wisdom of our fathers, precept by precept, until we would hunger for the truth of Christ.

Oh, thank You for these men of vision and understanding! Dear Pete, beyond the skies, will you petition the Father for his patience if we stumble?

There had been conferences before. The first at Pink, Oklahoma, but it was not really a conference so much as an in-gathering—an exploration of possibilities. As the cars and campers rolled onto the campgrounds and the people began to assemble, there was mounting excitement. How many there were! From Oklahoma the Cherokee, the Choctaw, and the Delaware. From Nebraska, the Omaha...oh, we couldn't count them all! The old, rich in tradition; the young, full of vitality; and the children, oh, the precious children. Then, at last, one of my own. Oh, children of mine, so scattered from each other, so close in spirit! This dear daughter and son, their family and his mother—the Navajo were here!

From the first, it was plain that this was to be a new kind of ministry. There were songs and prayers in various languages; it did not matter whether we could understand the words, our spirits spoke to one another in a universal language. We had been apart; now we were together, and nothing would ever be the same again. Not only for Indians was it a historic occasion; many people from the World Church who had hoped for and dreamed of this fulfillment were there. How many prayers and been lifted, how many searching questions about the result when at last the Lord would call the remnant to its awakening! I had told many of them, "It is going to be different. It may not be at all what you have expected." Now it was plain that one result would be a reaffirmation of faith, a revitalization of witness in this dream so long delayed.

There had been, subsequently, the gigantic conference in the Auditorium at Independence. The Parade of Nations at the convocation was impressive and colorful. The corridors were thronged with people, Indian and non-Indian alike converging upon an idea. The Navajo were there in force, and the prayers and songs in their ancient tongue lent a special beauty to the service. Now there were Sioux and Blackfeet, Algonquin, Cree, Athabascan and Mohawk.

Individual names began to replace tribal identities; strong ties developed, so that if one should ever be absent from our company, that one would be missed. Dear Ellen Stanley moved us all to tears with the Lord's Prayer in sign language, proving once more that even without words or mutual language the power of prayer is universal.

That was a conference-type conference with seminars, workshops, talent-sharing time, and good fellowship. We were overwhelmed by the unfamiliarity of such a massive event. We were a little frightened, I think, by so much love after the generations of withdrawal. We went apart and joined our hands; and we prayed that our hearts and the hearts of our people might be opened to receive such love and radiate it back again.

Now, called by Roland Williston, the minister-in-charge, the Eagles were to gather from across the land. Perhaps it was because we were under the open sky with our feet on the beloved earth, but we felt a new spirit. It was as though the Sacred Hoop had turned into position and was hovering above our heads, ready to bring us closer into the shelter of his love.

I had been immersed in worldly affairs; there had been too many meetings in too many formal settings, and I was disoriented during the first evening. I looked at the schedule—a simple thing with most of the items listed: "To be announced." The only activities that seemed to be firm were the Sweat Lodge in the morning and evening—and meals. Since the Sweat Lodge is not customarily open to women in my own culture, I was confused about what I would be doing, except to eat! Thursday evening we simply greeted old friends, watched for the next arrival, had a sing along—and ate.

Friday morning there seemed to be something we were supposed to do; but having gathered for breakfast we became so engrossed with talking and reaching out to one another that, before we knew it, lunch was being served. This was truly operating on Indian time (which means, actually, when the spirit moves us). The thing that most impressed me was how quickly the robe of "civilization" slipped from me; how neatly I slipped out of the time-structured world and became "one of the people" again.

Time is not a conveyor belt moving us inexorably through infancy, youth, and old age. Time is a river where we may dabble our feet, plunge into the rapids, or simply sit on the bank and dream.

Friday afternoon the Spirit moved on the river.

We trooped eagerly down into the valley where the most colossal tepee we had ever seen was waiting for us. Sixty-five feet long were the lodge poles that supported it. They had sprung from seeds on the floor of a canyon and had grown straight and tall, reaching for the sun. We walked about, measuring it with our eyes, breathless with the wonder of it. And I—who am always so full of words—was speechless.

I was a child again, standing on a bluff above the Mackenzie River flats, watching other Indian children at their play. Would hands once more reach out to pull me back from the place I longed to be?

As in a dream I looked at the playing field nearby, the players intent on their game. I heard the sounds of traffic on the street above the hill. I turned my back and bent to face the open entrance. I stepped inside—and was at home, at last. There was a different glow of light within the tepee; the sun was there but muted to a golden mist. The walls surrounded me like a mother's arms. The sides sloped gently inward and my eyes were lifted up to where one patch of sky reminded me of higher realms.

It was a precious, private time...a time to live once more the dream that brought me over all the miles and years to this one place, this point in time.

We took our places on the rows of chairs—those of us who knew that our world would be changed for us in this thing we were about to do, and those who were only waiting to see what would be done. This was to be, it was apparent, no fancy dress ball. Gone were the trappings, the pow-wow apparel; there were no drums. Here, it was plain, there would be one star—the Holy Spirit.

The center fire was lit not with elaborate ceremony but gently, one shaving, one twig, one branch at a time. Time? There was no sense of time. Man measures time; in eternity, there is no time.

The spiritual leaders entered, circling the fire, moving to sit quietly in their places on the blanket beyond it. The simple words, the words impressive beyond any oratory.

"What I am about to do is not done for the people but for the Great Spirit."

Of course. Worship is not for man, but man for God.

The firm, deliberate hands withdrawing the pipe from its beautiful bag—its presentation to the four directions.

Of course, brother Eagles! For the power of the Eternal Spirit extends to the ends of the earth.

The aromatic smell of cedar and sweetgrass filled the smoke-prayers that rose like incense. The call for the men of the nations who one by one rose from their places to sit in the circle of peace. *Hold the pipe firmly; touch it with deliberation; bathe in the incense and become part of your prayers and commitment.*

Oh, brothers! There are tribes beyond our knowledge

who are lost to one another; reach to them.

I think we all lost track of any sequence of events. What transpired one day or another was less important than what happened. Somewhere along there we had a business meeting, and it is noteworthy to record that we set our own rules for that, too. The only item of business was to adopt or amend a charter prepared by the Council. There was a brief discussion, a vote was called, and someone rose with another suggestion. A voice called "Point of order!" There was silence. Another brief discussion followed on the Rules of Order, then someone said, "I vote we pitch out Roberts and his rules of order. All we have to do is find out how we feel about the charter, so let's talk."

Someone said, "I vote we adopt the charter and think about it for a year." The vote was seconded. The business meeting passed on to higher things. I wish the Senators would take note and toss out the "rules of order" so they could get something done, for goodness' sake!

Every nation represented there knew such problems as would cause the strongest heart to quail. And yet the spoken prayers were not for blessings for themselves or favors. They prayed for other tribes whose problems were greater than their own. They prayed for the healing of division among the tribes of humankind; they prayed for earth—that the foolish and misled would let it stand until the purpose of the Lord should set the seal in his own time.

Here were Christians and Traditionalists lifting their prayers together in a harmony of spirit in the ancient way. Would the church which sponsored this remember that in that ancient time when history was halted for the remnant the burnt offering was still the sacred ritual ordained in times more ancient still?

Young Priest sitting quietly upon your blanket, waiting for the voice within to say, "It is time—I am ready," it is not alone the hands upon your head that confirm your office but the spirit within that says, "I accept." I think that all the ancients of our people would smile and nod in satisfaction to see you there, a Bible and the Pipe held in your hands.

They asked me why I chose this church and how my dream began. I took them through the years as, in the pages of this book, I've taken you. The lonely separation, the poverty and fear; the blessing of the loving hands stretched forth so long ago. I traced the years I'd spent in Washington, patting hands and drying tears while all our hopes came trembling to a close. Well maybe, as some people say, this was no time to wax political, but every Indian there knew what I meant when I said of that harrowing time: "My tears were for my people and their hopes; my tears were for my country and my shame."

This fair and blessed land, conceived in noble plan, held bound by chains of blind ambition, fear and unfledged dreams. Oh, Lord, preserve this holy earth that knew your loving touch. Imbue the spirits of those in power with vision and humility to know that you are in command. Teach them the ways of peace, and let them touch the earth with gentle hands.

On wings of prayer we flew beyond the pain.

By the meaning of the Pipe,
In Gospel Bonds

CHAPTER 20

For the Healing of the Nations

My beloved people:

I speak to you from a part of the country that many of your ancestors knew and loved. Here there are still great trees shading paths that knew the feet of many nations. Here in ancient times came many of our ancestors to the place of the flint, and here was heard the voice of Thunderbird, the Messenger, bringing a clear directive from the Supreme Being that this would forever be neutral ground where all the nations could assemble in peace.

I speak particularly to those of you who have been fragmented, torn, and dispersed, for I have lived my life as a displaced person and I know the loneliness and pain of separation. But I speak as well to those who have been able somehow, through ages of persecution and despair, to hold together the fabric of their nations.

All my years, my heart has run to you. I see you proud and laughing in your pain. I see you take a sheep that you can ill afford and slaughter it to feed your neighbors. I see the precious dark-eyed children and the eager looking into life of all our youth. I know their anger and frustration, and I know the talent that cries out for self-expression. But best of all, I love you when I see you rise and shake your feathers, saying to the Almighty Father and to the world: "We are here!"

Virtually every book, from the first texts used in public schools to very scientific studies, rehashes the theory of the Bering Strait and presents the Indian as a primitive, bound for 25,000 years in the rut of a stone-age culture. This is a danger to our people, for if the historians can convince us—or convince the world—that we were so stagnant, so lacking in creative skill or initiative or industry, that in all those years we made no advance in any way, do you see that it permits those who wish us ill to excuse themselves for their persecutions and say, "Well, after all, they were hardly men."

Instead, we know that our people have had a long and varied history. There have been peaks and valleys, times when powerful nations arose, and times when they fell.

Our concern in these last generations has been with the terrible period of our contact with European cultures. When we regard the sorry conditions of our nations, it is understandable that we long for the days when we lived a simpler life. Looking back, it seems that period must have been a paradise of hunting and fishing and living peacefully in the gentle arms of Mother Earth. But I have wandered the byways of our history. I have followed our ancestors through long migrations preserved as dim traditions. To stand upon the mountaintop and look back down the valley is to view many features of the landscape we do not see walking along the path. In the journey on which my research took me I found many strange things not to be found in the history books. I found, for instance, that there were evidences of close contact with the civilizations of

Central and South America. I found traditions describing the migrations of ancient ancestors from those places. If this is true, as it seems to be, somewhere among us are the children of the Sun Kings whose genius built those fabulous cities to the south.

I found several versions of an ancient prophecy, well known to our great-grandfathers. There have been occasional hints in the accounts of early explorers and settlers that our ancestors were not too surprised to see strange people coming upon our shores.

The legend that precedes the prophecy is told in different words sometimes, but the meaning seems plain: in some far ancient time there was a period of such constant and unrelenting warfare that the land ran red with blood.

In sorrow, the Great Spirit looked down at his children. He had not placed them on earth to quarrel with one another. He wanted them to live in peace, for the land was vast and could be shared by all. Still the wars continued. The game which fed the people fled before the noise of battle. There was much misery. Then, angrily, the Great Spirit looked on the warring tribes and spoke to them in the voice of thunder!

> This is my fair land; with my hands and my heart have I made it, and it is dearer to me than all the lands of earth. If you cannot live by my laws, sharing in peace the gifts I have given, then I will cause such enemies as you have never seen to come upon you. They will put their feet upon your necks and grind your faces in the dust.

Then, however, in his love and mercy the Great Spirit made a promise:

> Some far day it will happen that you will begin to lift your heads. You will remember the wisdom of your fathers, and you will climb to the top of the mountain and stretch wide your arms, saying, "Father, we are here!"—and I will remember.

My people, something wonderful *is* happening in the

world of the Indian. A feeling of brotherhood, like the first breath of spring, has begun to spread across the land southward and the land North. It is no formal organization; it is beyond that. It is a mere fanning of the breeze as yet; but it will sweep like a mighty wind, blowing away the foolish factions and divisions.

In these days we have begun to remember and to seek the ways of our fathers, and we are remembering the ancient covenant which the Great Spirit made with them that this day would come. We have survived a time in our history when, by all the rules of statistics, we should have become extinct. We are still here. Though there are still factions and divisions, complaints and dissatisfactions, we have begun to reach out to one another to acknowledge as never before our brotherhood.

If ever in the history of the world there was proof of the constancy of the Creator's covenant with his people, it is manifest in the Indian. Let us, with confidence in the eternal love of the Creator, look up in peace and commit ourselves to him.

So now we begin to assemble our nations. The scattered remnants that dropped off along the path of our dispersion once more seek the shelter of the wings of their nations. Many of our people have been the unwilling victims of separation. Many of them have little knowledge of the customs and traditions, the rituals or the social structure of their fathers. It is the will of the Creator in this time of the fulfillment of the prophecy that those who have had the good fortune to preserve even a seed of their memories begin now to nourish that seed...with the rain of truth. They should not accept the interpretation of scholars, no matter how learned they may be, but look deep within the old traditions for their roots. And to instruct those who return—not in pride, but with compassion.

We have always lived with prophecy and dreams, so in this time of fulfillment we must realize that each event in our history has been in some way involved in this promise—a preparation of our people for a great destiny. If we look far into the ancient past of our fathers, before the white men came, and if we recognize the brotherhood of those within the seven races, we shall see that our tradition embraced a great variety of life-styles. Let no one accept the childish idea that in order to be a real Indian, he has to live in a tepee and wash clothes in a stream. Remember that among the ancestors were those who built great irrigation systems and made wise laws for their people. Remember, too, that before the white men came, many of our tribes were forced by more powerful bands to change their locations. People from the gentle climate of the South were driven to the harshness of the North, and people from the woodlands to the plains. What that added to our natures was a great resilience, an ability to adapt to new and hard conditions. This took imagination and creative skill.

Though our ancient history was filled with division and strife, and those mighty nations dwindled into scattered bands, the Great Spirit was able to shape even this sorry course of events into the final design. Survival in the natural world required strength, hard work, and courage. This was built into our very bones through countless generations. Thus, in this framework, there should be room for the talents we have acquired in these last centuries.

Most of us who have lived with any contact with our white neighbors have found many who are sympathetic toward our people. True, they are uninformed about just where our difficulties lie, and we are often impatient when they do not bother to inquire, but there are two facts of which we should be aware. Even those who manifest interest find that very little information is available to the public; and they, too, are caught in a web of circumstance with problems that they have inherited and problems that have developed in a very complex society. Nevertheless, they are our neighbors. To truly remember the ways of our fathers is to be sensitive to their needs. What our white neighbors need is quietness of spirit, a knowledge of the permanence of life. We can make a better world both for ourselves and them if we witness of our age-old wisdom in these things. Then, let the young listen to the teachings of the elders and, as they move out into the world, carry with them that security of mind which will bind the wounds of their companions. We complain that we are tired of waiting for someone to bring something to us. What we have to give is far more precious, far more essential, than any material improvement the world has to offer.

It is possible that we may continue to live in the white man's world, but not of it. For the present, just as we ask that we be allowed to live according to our belief, to worship in our own manner, so must we recognize the right of others to pursue happiness in their own way. If we gain this right and grant the same to others, it will be a new thing; for always in the past, arrogance has decreed, "My way is right; therefore, your way is wrong." If we are large-souled enough to say, "My way is right for me; your way is right for you; let there be peace between us," we shall do what no one has done before.

There are vast questions to be resolved if we are to heal our wounds, and many of them involve the statement of our individual and various faiths. It is not my purpose here to explain or define the doctrines of those among us who include in their worship a reverence for Jesus Christ. To Christians, some experience or training in their lives has led them into a relationship with One whom they believe to be the very Son of God. Their faith is precious to them, but I think it does not make them less Indian, for many of our ancestors paid reverence to the Prince of Heaven, Lord of the Dawn, and God of Wind and Water.

In the increasing tide of the resurgence of our spirit as a people, we are often torn by internal strife. This is not good. Let us beware lest we fall into the same pattern that so divided and weakened our nations in the past. Many hundreds of years ago the Iroquois Nations and the various confederacies knew that these quarrels within and between nations were self-defeating. We know that there are outside forces that would keep us divided and make full and effective use of tensions between urban and reservation Indians, between Christian Indians and Traditionalists. Let us not assist them to divide us further.

Let us certainly not be divided about a name that has come to us from another of the languages of the earth. Few of our nations are known by the names originally held, yet we know who we are. Sioux, Oneida, Creek, Delaware—these are names that have developed through contact with another race, but we answer to them and accept them. So it should be in our worship of God. Let there be no quarreling between us because of the name by which God is addressed. He knows who we mean, in whatever language we address him, as long as our hearts speak to him truly.

It took the passage of a new law to affirm that we had the right to practice our religion. Although the experience of many had led us to the belief that our various religions were offensive to other faiths, many Indians can testify that it was never the will of all American people that this privilege should be denied. Nevertheless, that denial did exist among small-minded people and it was a great sin, a violation of the principle of freedom of worship in this country. Now that the question has been resolved, there should be no criticism of our brothers who express their worship in a manner different from our own. To do so would be to commit a sin we have condemned.

By the same token, those of us who attempt to follow Christ must know that as Christians, we cannot judge our brothers, for according to Christ's words, all are the sheep of his pasture. The rituals and ceremonies were given to us because they expressed our own national experiences and occasions of thanksgiving and praise. They are good and no more to be denied to any Indian, whether Christian or Traditionalist, than should be the joyful festival of Christmas. All—*all* are expressions of prayer or joyous thanksgiving.

Let us remember the words of our Creator to our people in the days of our youth:

> Verily, I say there are two kinds of minds on earth. One follows true those things I have ordained of love and kindness to each other. One follows after things of darkness, with no love of peace, the bat-thoughts of my brother, Tawiskaron.

Let the wounds be healed—now! Let us get on with firm steps to the top of our mountain.

For each of our nations the difficulties, the aims and purposes of their own people have been the prime consideration, for problems have differed according to region, resources, and relationships with the white community. We look back with bitter anger on the terrible wrongs done to our people and to our beloved land. Our anger often increases when we see ignorance or arrogance or indifference binding us in a prison of frustration. But now, for the first time in centuries, windows are opening. Education and self-direction are beginning to be available to bring new life to our people—if we will use our energy to stretch forth our hands to take them.

The purpose of the Creator for this earth is peace and joy and fulfillment for each of his children. The promise he made was very sure. Though we grieve for those who died along the way, let us give thanks to him for the preservation of the seeds of our nations; for neither the armies of Spanish, French, English, and Dutch, nor any combination of circumstances has been able to extinguish our race.

Now every life is precious. Let the dreary statistics of suicide among our people cease. Let the curse of alcohol and drugs be put from us; for we must be about a noble project, and we need clear minds to attain it.

One of the most serious divisions within the nations had been the controversy between elected and Traditional chiefs, and it is the one that can most speedily be healed if we truly remember the ways of our fathers.

A little consideration about the problems facing our people today shows that we must choose leaders who have knowledge of the law (or at least who are able to deal with a legal situation), and people who understand road-building, health services, schools, land titles. This is not only common sense but the law if we are to have the funds and services so vital to our communities.

On the other hand, no group of leaders ever lived who had more influence over the moral ethic of their people than did the Traditional chiefs. It was the time-honored tradition of our fathers to have both war chiefs and peace chiefs, and I think it is within our knowledge that the greatest Sachems were never known to the outside world. The value of this system was that these good men were able to sit in council together, each adding his wisdom in his particular role for the good of the people.

One of the most valid purposes in seeking greater control in our tribal governments should be the establishing of a viable role for the Traditional chiefs. Today we have the elected chiefs who are responsible for waging battles with day-to-day problems in our communities. Let the influence of the peace chiefs be to sustaining the moral health of our people, of the guarding of the best traditions that they not pass from memory. Let them be accorded equal honor and be equally concerned with the peace of the nation.

Love, respect, honor, and brotherhood cannot be legislated away. These are the things people cherish in their heart, and unless we are able to hold fast these things it is foolish for us to talk about "the Indian way."

I believe that it has been no accident that our feet still walk the earth. There is a depth and height to the spirits of our people that will one day be a blessing on the earth. There is a power of darkness loose among the tribes of men that only strong wills can withstand. Somewhere within the memories of our nations is the hidden meaning of all life on the earth. When we find it, it will bring a healing to all nations so that we and they will mount as eagles to the mountaintop of peace.

Be strong!

EPILOGUE

The Kingdom

One of the early agents among the Wyandot reported that he had seen some very old wampum which the Indians described as "a message from the emperor of the South." Interpreting it, they claimed that it was a warning to the people of the North that a strange beast had appeared upon the emperor's shores, having the body of a man but the four legs of a beast. In its hands it held an instrument that poured forth thunder and lightning; it was very dangerous, and he was thus sending a warning to his brothers. The story suggests that the landing of the Spanish in Central America was not unknown to the people of the North.

An interesting legend was told by David Cusick, an early convert to Christianity. His manner of delivering it demonstrates why, in the old days, traditions were transmitted in chants that had to be patiently learned word for word. To change them might put forth an entirely false premise.

His story began, "Many years ago—oh, maybe two thousand years before the white man came..."

This was obviously an attempt either to impress or to please the white missionaries, for such tales never began with an identification of time. There would have been nothing beyond the statement that such an event occurred "once, long ago," or "long before the time of our grandfather's grandfathers."

The rest of the legend was told simply enough. It was a story of a newly chosen young chief of one of the tribes of the Great Lakes region. He had a desire *to go and see* the golden cities and to visit the emperor of the South. He chose a party of warriors and they traveled southward. They did at last see the emperor and marveled at the gold. Returning home they were astonished and very much alarmed to see that the land was fortified almost to the Great Lakes. They hastened to warn their people and to prepare for war.

There are several interesting points in this brief tale which has been analyzed and discounted by historians. The language of tradition is explicit, for only so could true history be passed from one generation to another. It is, in fact, almost impossible to deviate from the old pattern once the tale is well begun. Granting that Cusick made that one slip in mentioning a date, I think he then told the legend as it had been told to him, without embroidery.

The young chief "desired to go and see." He did not set out to explore or to check if a story told around the campfire were true. He had a definite goal in mind—to see the emperor of the South and the golden cities. Obviously he must have had good reason to believe they were there.

Historians have also cast doubt about the gold; the northeastern Indian was not supposed to know about gold. Perhaps he was confusing gold with mica which decorated many of the mounds, they said. It is rather pointless to assume that the young chief would confuse mica with gold. Even assuming that gold was not a valued commodity among Indians, mica was well-known. Perhaps the legend means what it says.

On his return he was impressed with the fortifications (one wonders by what route he traveled that he did not see them on the journey south). Particularly through the Ohio valley and, in fact, throughout all the states east of the Mississippi, there were great complexes of mounds and earthworks—except, that is, east of the Alleghenies.

Nor can we be certain that the fortifications belonged to those who were arming them, for the migration stories of the Iroquois and the Leni-Lenape told of great battles fought with the so-called Moundbuilders who were driven out or exterminated in the process. The Cherokee, whom early antiquarians designated as the descendants of the "Allegwi"—those legendary earth builders—insisted that the mound cities were deserted when their ancestors entered the territory *from the south*.

If we proceed with this reasoning we may almost be persuaded that these northern tribes had some knowledge of the southland, its emperors, and its golden cities. Yet here they were, subsisting by hunting and gathering, accepting with monumental patience the hard facts of wilderness life. For though we like to glamorize it, life in those days *was* hard. It was no life for the weak or the insecure.

So why, if they knew of these great cultures, why in the name of conscience did they not adopt some of the comforts, build roads to travel on, and houses of stone to protect them from those wintry blasts?

The question haunted me many years; for when I first became aware of history I became enchanted, like the young chief of this story, with the golden cities of the South. It has taken me a long time to see a connection, and all the tale is not yet told. More and more each day memories are being awakened, old songs sung, old legends told. If the implication proves true, then the Northern American Indians accomplished in their history what men have been threatening to do since the dawn of civilization—and did it so well that even today when all the delights and comforts of civilization are offered to them they feel some uneasiness, some sense of wanting to pick and choose which things will be compatible with their concept of the good life.

It is as though—if we can believe the tales of great migrations from the South—in some far time the ancestors deliberately turned their backs on those golden cities and all they represented. It is as though they *chose* this ascetic life and pruned away all knowledge of that other world, leaving alone a pure and shining faith in the great Maker and the fierce will to survive.

It seemed to me one time that all those cities to the south were a paradise where beautiful, sophisticated people lived in splendor. While the ancestors of Britain roamed the forests and painted their faces blue, the Inca ate from lavish plates and drank from jeweled cups. They spun a cotton finer than the sheerest linen and played music worthy of a Bach. The Maya and the Toltec raised their mighty pyramids and measured time. They built great roads and temples shining in the sun; and all of them sent out great colonies to spread their empires.

It should have been so beautiful, but under all the panoply of wealth and power a stain of blood swept out. The bloody gods drank up the flood, and wars were fought to bring them more. The thirst for power set each ruler's hand against his neighbor king, and then at last his feet upon the necks of his own subjects.

In all the land there was but one gentle memory, and even this was being lost in the great lust for blood. One gentle memory of a pure and holy one who came to teach them how to live with honor. He said that he would come again...but oh, the centuries were long! The people wearied, lost their hope, their very lives until—the rulers could not hold them and they slipped away, away into the friendly wilderness where all they had to fear were cold, and rain, and wind.

Never, never again would they trust man's lust for power. Trust God, trust the earth; trust their own strength and skill—but never man when he builds with power.

Then, when the wilderness gates had closed and the wise men assembled the tales that were safe for the telling, there developed a people who grew strong in spirit. There was nothing between man and the Great One but the air, and through it the smoke of his prayers rose straight as an arrow.

Then there came to the southland men of a different race, with a lust for power to match that of the rulers...with weapons that drank more blood than the gods ever dreamed of. With them came the long-robes who told of the Son of God who had come to a land across the sea, who taught love and brotherhood and forgiveness.

"We know," said the people, weeping, "for he came to us."

"Slay them!" screamed the long-robes. "Cut out their tongues; for surely this is the devil's own work."

"He will come again," said the ruler. "See, we have kept his throne ready, and he will be our king. Now we are sorry for our misdeeds. Here are the books of the records. Come, let us study together and prepare for the Lord of the Dawn."

But the books were burned; the emperor was killed; and another kingdom was established.

When will the human race learn the majesty of the Creator and know that his promises were given to all people that they, meeting at some far day, might rejoice together?

Let us build a new legend.

* * * * *

Let us imagine a kingdom and over it as ruler a king—by divine right, by birth, and by the strength of his personality. He has planned and executed such laws as he feels wise for his people that their lives may be peaceful and productive. He has assembled architects and engineers and made available to them the tools and resources for the construction of great buildings, roads, and parks. He has caused teachers to be raised up for the instruction of the young and fostered libraries and laboratories for the increase of knowledge. The poor—for there are always the poor—he loves and hears their cries. But being wise, he does not pave their way with instant riches, for he knows that people thrive best by their own efforts, and that from challenge and necessity rise those of character and strength and vision.

There are taxes, of course, for all these benefits must be paid for; but the taxes are not greater than the people can bear, and for those who have not money certain services to the kindgom are quite acceptable. This, too, is wisdom; for how can it be his people's homeland unless they are involved in its building?

Now one would think that in such a kingdom joy would reign supreme, that all would love this wise and gentle king. This is not so, for there is much dissension. This, too, is permitted; for the ruler has decreed that his subjects must be free to think their own thoughts and to voice them; that a decent amount of change is necessary as people grow older in knowledge.

Still, there are those who differ with his policy—the greedy who would funnel into their own pockets funds for health and education; the ignorant who think this thirst for knowledge is a silly pursuit; the lazy who think it is too hard. There are those who resent the laws and would rather make their own—and those who want no law at all.

Besides—across the border is another king who daily grows richer and more powerful; and it is said that over there, one can get away with anything. There the whole aim of life is to eat, drink, and be merry, and the entire populace is occupied twenty-four hours a day in those pursuits. It is an attractive prospect to many who find the words "duty" and "responsibility" a bit dull.

Possibly the most dangerous of all, however, are those within the king's own court who feel that because they "have his ear" he belongs exclusively to them. If the ruler goes out incognito, as he often does, to sit with the people in their gardens or among their children, his courtiers secretly sigh that it would be better if he left such things to them and attended to weightier matters. If he stays within his office, his ministers often go about shouting, "Thus saith the King," and proclaim nonsense that would never have crossed his mind.

So it is obvious that this "king by divine right" has problems with his people. But two things are certain: he is not deluded, and he *is* the king. He is king over the courtiers and over the poorest peasant in the fields. He is king over those who love and honor him, and over those who belittle and disobey him.

He *is* the king.

So, it would seem, is the situation in the kingdom of God. So it has been with his Son, born to be Lord of the Dawn and King of the Earth. He sat with us in our homes and gardens, and became a dear and valued friend, a precious Elder Brother, wise and gentle, kind and open-hearted, after whom we took our pattern— though we failed to reach his stature. Many princes rose to claim him: "He is ours, He has proclaimed it!"

Evil men have lured away many children of the kingdom to the service of that other ruler; and they find that all the license of the senses turns at last to dust and ashes. Bodies tortured by a thirst they cannot quench, nerves and intellect embattled and destroyed; and the laughter of their pretender king adds fuel to their despair.

Perhaps in our desire for a close personal relationship with this great Prince of heaven we may forget his majesty, his universal message. We may see him only as *our* friend, *our* own dear teacher. Thus in time it seems that he becomes "the Catholic Christ," "The Protestant Christ," "the White Man's Christ," or the Rejuvenator of Wovoka, or the God of Wind and Water of the South—but not all.

How can we limit him, the holy emissary of that almighty, universal God whose works no one on earth can fully understand. Scholars spend their lives seeking the truth about a single species and admit that there is more to learn. What kind of God was this who made them all, who ordered molecules and planets, and whose natural laws still function in one eternal plan of order out of chaos? A little God locked up in Sinai...one whose spirit spread across a universe of stars and suns and reached into the tiniest crevice of the earth?

Of one thing we may be sure—he does not do his work halfway, but in full measure, packed and running over. Abraham, in his love for God, prepared to sacrifice his son and saw him lifted up to become the father of uncounted millions. But the almighty Father of the Universe, to show his love for all, sacrificed the Prince of Heaven and raised him up—the king.

We have dreamed of such a king, ruling in love at some far day, someday when certain things "have come to pass," when by some miracle the earth would cleanse itself of all pollution. From north to south, from east to west across the earth, men have waited through the centuries, daring to believe, losing hope, daring to believe again.

Perhaps at last we should proclaim that all this while he *has been* king, and only we have been good, bad, or indifferent subjects of his kingdom.

Sweep clean his temples and his courts and deck them anew with honesty and truth. Open wide the windows, let the fresh air blow in all the dusty corners. Wash the children's faces, dry their tears, and make them smile. Bind the wounds and break the chains of all the slaves of ignorance and avarice. Now there is no wilderness where humankind may hide and nurse its wounds. Here, here on this sacred land—scarred though it be—the healing must begin. For when the Elder Brother comes, that long-awaited Holy One, what legend will be told about our time...if there be time at all?

"The ancestors were cruel and thoughtless men. 'My profits, my possessions' was their creed. They lived with secret or with open hate, nor cared about the tears of children, or the heart-hunger of their fellowman.

Pollution and decay followed where they walked. Thus, when He came, that Dawn-Lord they had ceased to hope for, they were much ashamed. Their tears fell on the scarred, unlovely earth."

Or will they say, "There came a day when, weary with getting and spending, with bowing beneath the lash, sick unto death of the lust for power, the ancestors stood upright and looked with clear eyes at their world. Each one faced the wilderness within and sought that portion of the Creator's spirit that enabled him to do good and not evil. To presidents and senators and potentates and premiers and all the courtiers around their thrones, they said:

"You are our temporal leaders and we offer such respect as you have earned. But we expect our king—the king of all the earth—of those bound either by their own ignorance or arrogance as well as those whose spirits have learned freedom in his truth. And we *will* have laws and courts and programs that befit his kingdom. We *will* have more of statesmanship and less of politics. We *will* have less of shady deals and more of righteous plan. We *will* have unpolluted streams, good air to breathe; and if we have to learn once more to use our legs, so let it be. We *will* have more attention given to reclaim waste places of the earth, and more respect for the right of all his creatures to survive.

"We will not flee again but stand in faith and hope, with clear eyes and with eager hearts after the long waiting."

And thus, at last, they spread a royal purple carpet for the coming of the King.

THE BEGINNING

— — — — — —

There will be a brief intermission before the last act in which the Star invites the audience to participate. He also extends an invitation for any who desire to meet with him for refreshment on the mezzanine after the final curtain.